Cravings Made Vegan

Cravings Made Vegan

50 Plant-Based Recipes for Your Comfort Food Favorites

Bianca Haun & Sascha Naderer

Skyhorse Publishing

Skyhorse Publishing books may be purchased in bulk at special discounts for sales promotion, corporate gifts, fund-raising, or educational purposes. Special editions can also be created to specifications. For details, contact the Special Sales Department, Skyhorse Publishing, 307 West 36th Street, 11th Floor, New York, NY 10018 or info@skyhorsepublishing.com.

Visit our website at www.skyhorsepublishing.com.

10 9 8 7 6 5 4 3 2

Library of Congress Cataloging-in-Publication Data is available on file.

Cover design by Jenny Zemanek
Cover photo by Bianca Haun and Sascha Naderer

Print ISBN: 978-1-5107-3932-1
Ebook ISBN: 978-1-5107-3933-8

Printed in China

Our goal is not to create more vegans, but to create more vegan options for ourselves, for our families, for our friends, and for you, so we dedicate this book to everyone who wants to contribute to change. Step by step, meal by meal.

TABLE OF CONTENTS

HI!

IT'S US (AGAIN)

We're Bianca and Sascha, a foodie couple who went vegan and decided to share our creations with the world. After publishing *The Veginner's Cookbook: The Ultimate Starter Guide for New Vegans and the Veg-Curious* to help vegan beginners adjust to their new lifestyle, the idea for this book, a more advanced cookbook for every vegan who deals with non-vegan cravings, was born.

After following a vegan diet for two years, I (Bianca) started sharing my favorite plant-based recipes on the blog *Elephantastic Vegan* (ElephantasticVegan.com). Since then, I have shared hundreds of plant-based recipes, a handful of vegan travel reports, kitchen hacks, product reviews, and guides for new and experienced vegans. Born and raised in Austria, a meat-focused country like so many, I want to prove that a vegan diet is not just possible, but that it can also be tasty and decadent.

Sascha is a lover of food that cooks itself, so all kinds of soups, stews, goulashes, and curries are usually his area of expertise. Taking basic meat alternatives to the next tasty level is also kind of his thing. He's not into baking and using step-by-step recipes, but he will gladly gobble down all the baked goods he can find. Showing people how delicious plant-based food can be is his favorite way of sparking people's interest in a vegan diet.

AN INTRODUCTION

WE ARE VEGANS, AND WE HAVE NON-VEGAN CRAVINGS

It's hard to find a vegan who doesn't (sometimes) crave non-vegan foods, so why is it so easy to feel bad about it? Chances are, you weren't born a vegan. For most vegans, veganism is a conscious choice made at some point during our lives. Before going vegan, you probably experienced many BBQs with friends, pancake Sundays with family, or drunken Saturday night grilled-cheese sandwiches at 4 a.m. Many of us associate some of our best and dearest memories with specific tastes, and it can be hard to let those tastes go.

So, we decided we wouldn't. In our first cookbook, *The Veginner's Cookbook*, we addressed how to get through the various landmine situations in which the temptation to eat non-vegan foods is strong, but remember, it's still okay to crave. You are not the first vegan to crave the non-vegan stuff. We ultimately decided that feeling sorry about our cravings is no longer an option—but creating awesome alternatives is. Our constant drive to experiment and vega-nize well-known classics is such a fun and adventurous task for us that we decided to share some of our favorite ways to feast in this book.

Cheese fries. Lasagna. Philly cheesesteak. Shawarma. Mac & cheese. Corn dogs. Panna cotta. Donuts. This is not a book about healthy people eating salad. These are Cravings. Made. Vegan.

Part 1

SUBSTITUTE EVERYTHING: THE MAGICAL INGREDIENTS FOR VEGANS

What was your first experience with tofu? If you're like us, the first slice you ever cooked was a bland, tasteless mess. What a turnoff. Yet, some people seem to make all tofu, soy protein, or even broccoli taste so good that you'll never want to eat meat again.

As former on-and-off vegetarians, we feel you. Your scrambled tofu gets tastier, but it's not eggs; your cheesy sauce is missing something; and whatever you try, nothing seems to come close to the smokiness of bacon. While some vegans don't mind at all, many people miss specific flavors so much that they eventually go back to their old non-vegan eating habits.

There's a good chance that you didn't go vegan because you hated chicken fingers, kebabs, or grilled cheese. The ethics of veganism is one of the most common reasons for people to adopt a vegan lifestyle. But we're also human, so non-vegan cravings are also common and entirely reasonable. That's why we're always eager to learn about new ways to veganize foods we love.

So, how can you go from an on-and-off vegetarian (who could never stop eating cheese because it's just so yummy) to a happy vegan that always has an alternative up their sleeves? We're here to help you fight the urge to order a cheese pizza or get yourself a treat of buttered popcorn. We've tried a million things to get our vegan food to the next level, and now we'd love to share a few magical ingredients to make your vegan diet awesome.

THE MEAT ALTERNATIVES AND HOW TO BACON

If you're looking to substitute meat, there are many great choices, the obvious and most well-known being tofu. However, you should give other options such as tempeh or seitan a try. For maximum protein, check out textured vegetable protein, which comes in different shapes and sizes and can be used to substitute (almost) every product. For a chicken or pork taste, you can't go wrong with everything related to paprika, garlic, and salt. If you want to go for a beefier taste, try deglazing your meat alternatives with a mix of red wine, soy sauce, and liquid smoke.

What's liquid smoke, you ask? Some hate it, but for many vegans, it is one of the best ways to recreate an intense smoky flavor. It's usually sold in small bottles, but the liquid is so potent that you'll only need a small amount for each dish. Tofu, tempeh, or soy protein all benefit from the smoky flavor that comes from marinating or seasoning with liquid smoke. You've heard about tempeh bacon for your pizza, but yours taste like nothing? Liquid smoke. Your soy granule tastes boring? Liquid smoke. Missing that extra oomph in your chili? Oh, my, liquid smoke!

Finding the perfect fish and seafood alternatives can be tricky. We recommend mixing tofu with a seaweed, such as nori, and round it off with something like lemon, dill, and capers to fight sudden seafood cravings.

HOW DO YOU LIKE YOUR EGGS?

Eggs are not as crucial in baking as you might think, so this one's easy: replace with baking powder, mashed bananas, or apple purée. Chia or flax eggs (mix 1 tablespoon of ground chia/flax seeds with 3 tablespoons water and let sit for 20 minutes to replace 1 egg) are also great substitutes for eggs in both sweet and savory baked goods. If you're looking for an alternative to cooking with eggs, tofu is your friend. Just make sure to try out different kinds of tofu for different textures. We suggest using soft to regular tofu for scrambling and silken tofu for eggy spreads. If you're not into tofu, you can use avocados for spreads or even the pulp of a fresh, young Thai coconut.

A key ingredient for everything eggy is kala namak or Himalayan black salt. Kala namak is most commonly used in Indian cuisine, but we call it the egg maker. While it's violet to black in its rock form, it turns into a pinkish color when ground. What is this sorcery? Kala namak has a high sulfur content, resulting in an eggy taste and smell on whatever it's sprinkled on. (Just make sure you go easy on other salts because kala namak is salt itself.) So, if you're missing that little something extra in your tofu scramble or avocado spreads, try kala namak.

MAKE EVERYTHING CHEESY WITH NUTRITIONAL YEAST

There are whole books and blogs dedicated to creating all kinds of vegan cheese, so if you need inspiration for a difficult endeavor like this, make sure to check out vegan cheese makers online such as Miyoko Schinner. To get you started, silken tofu can help you achieve a cheesy texture. You can also blend some almonds, cashews, or walnuts to create an excellent base for vegan cheese.

Nutritional yeast is another great ingredient with a cheesy taste. Nutritional yeast is simply deactivated yeast that you can buy as a powder or in flake form. It's super popular among vegans because it has an interesting cheesy flavor. It's a perfect source of vitamin B, and if you're lucky, you can find a brand that fortifies its nutritional yeast with vitamin B_{12}. Use nutritional yeast for everything that should be cheesy. Create cheese sauces for pizza and lasagna, bake up some cheesy crackers, and sprinkle the stuff over pasta, risottos, or even popcorn. Once you try this, you will never have enough at home.

DON'T YOU DAIRY

Good news; it's super easy to switch out milk, yogurt, butter, or cream in most recipes. If you've never had anything but milk and dairy yogurt, try the plethora of plant-based drinks and yogurts made from soy, hemp, almond, cashew, hazelnut, coconut, rice, oat, or even pistachios and macadamia. You can use these drinks for your morning coffee and breakfast, for baking, and everything you would use milk or yogurt for. Try to experiment with the dishes you like most for your purpose; it's fun!

If you're looking for an alternative to butter, there's a variety of vegan butters available in stores made out of canola, avocado, or other plants. Coconut oil is another great alternative. Beware of margarine, which frequently contains animal products.

For heavy cream, try unsweetened coconut milk. For whipped cream, check out whipped coconut cream. If you're not into coconut, many stores offer a good variety of alternative products based on oats, rice, or soy.

HOW TO DEEP-FRY WITHOUT A DEEP-FRYER

There are many reasons not to have a deep-fryer; ours is the fear that a deep-fryer is the only thing keeping us from doubling our weight within the year. Whatever your reason is, if you feel like frying something once in a while, there's absolutely no need to buy yet another kitchen appliance. Here are some things to know before frying in a pot.

Type of oil: use oil with a high smoke point (e.g., canola oil, sunflower oil, peanut oil, or soybean oil).

Pot size: The smaller the pot, the less oil you will need. We always use the smallest pot possible for our soon-to-be-fried goods.

Oil amount: Fill the pot with just enough oil so that the food you want to fry can swim in the oil. Don't fill the pot more than ⅓ to ½ full with oil. If the oil rises too much when frying, a spill-over might happen, and that means trouble.

Oil temperature: The ideal temperature for the oil would be 375°F/190°C. Use a deep-fry thermometer if you have one. If not, stick the end of a wooden spoon into the oil; if it sizzles around the stick, it's hot enough. The oil should never smoke; if it does, reduce the heat.

Preparing the food: Make sure the foods you want to fry are patted dry before putting in the oil-filled pot. Water and oil are worst enemies.

Lowering the food into the oil: Make sure you carefully lower the food into the oil with a slotted deep-fry spoon or tongs to prevent hot oil splashes!

Frying times: Smaller foods will take less time to fry. If you notice that foods brown too quickly, but they are not done on the inside, lower the oil temperature. Never walk away from the pot when you fry. Just don't.

Removing excess oil: Transfer the fried goods onto a plate lined with paper towels to remove excess oil.

Save the oil: No need to toss out the oil after frying! Let it cool off completely, then strain the oil to remove solid bits and transfer it into a container to use several times over.

STOP MAKING CRAPPY VEGAN BURGERS

We'll never forget our first vegan burger. It was 2012 and we were vacationing in the US when we stumbled across a vegan restaurant in San Francisco. We were on-and-off vegetarians with no desire to say goodbye to cheese at the time, and veganism wasn't exactly big where we lived in Austria, so we were curious to try something new. We had this fantastic vegan cheeseburger, and it was right then and there that we decided going vegan might not be such a hard thing to pull off after all.

Little did we know that we were years away from being able to recreate anything remotely close to that vegan cheeseburger. For a long time, we had problems making decent burger patties that didn't fall apart completely. Our base was always too moist or crumbly, but never right, so after some trial and (lots of) error, we discovered the one ingredient that can save any burger recipe that never seems to be just right: rolled oats. Whether it's sweet potatoes, kidney beans, lentils, or even mushrooms, combine your base with rolled oats, and you've got one of the best possible binders. For texture, add nuts or sunflower seeds, and please season your burger. Actually, please, for your own sake, season your food in general. It sounds simple, but even veggie restaurants don't always get this right.

The proof is not just in the patty; the bread is essential, as well. If your poppy seeds or sesame seeds don't want to stick to the burger buns, brush the top with water or plant-based milk and then apply the seeds. The flour in the pieces of bread and the water will act as glue. If you want to add seeds after baking, we love to use water and a bit of maple syrup to make the top sticky enough.

Now that you've got your patty base and bread, fry your burger, get yourself some lettuce, and top everything off with an incredible vegan mayo or BBQ sauce. Add tomatoes? Sure. Onions? Go crazy. If you're into pickles, do pickles.

Done. Perfect burger.

Part II

THE MOST IMPORTANT THING IN LIFE? FAM . . . BREAKFAST

Have you noticed that so many vegan breakfast recipes you find online or in books are healthy or trying to act like it? There's nothing wrong with that. However, especially for the savory vegan, the constant stream of chia puddings and green smoothies in coffee shops and bars can be a dull and unappealing experience. There is a place for recipes like that. This book isn't it. In our breakfast section, we share our veganized takes on breakfast classics including everything from making eggs with silken tofu to cream cheese with almonds. And breakfast pizza.

TOFU SCRAMBLE ON RYE

Makes: *3 toasts* | Time: *20 min*

Using just a few special ingredients, you can take your tofu game to a whole new level. If you prefer savory meals and you've been feeling the breakfast blues since going vegan, this treat is going to make you fall in love with your first meal of the day all over again. Put this scramble on rye bread, add some vegan butter, and sprinkle on some fresh chives for maximum savory and eggy deliciousness.

INGREDIENTS

10 oz. (280 g) firm tofu

1 teaspoon canola oil

¼ teaspoon turmeric powder

¼ teaspoon curry powder

¾ teaspoon kala namak (Himalayan black salt)

4 tablespoons oat milk*

3 slices rye bread

vegan butter to spread on toast

1 teaspoon chives, chopped

INSTRUCTIONS

1. Scramble the tofu with your hands or a fork.
2. Heat the canola oil in a large pan and add in scrambled tofu.
3. Add the turmeric powder, curry powder, and kala namak. Mix well until the tofu takes on an even yellow color.
4. Add the oat milk and keep the pan on medium to high heat while stirring for about 7 minutes (or less if you prefer a mushier scramble). Add more kala namak to taste.
5. Spread vegan butter on the rye bread and add on your scrambled tofu. Sprinkle with fresh chives and enjoy. Faith in vegan breakfasts restored.

---

*Adding oat milk gives the tofu a soft eggy texture. You can omit the oat milk for a drier tofu scramble.

CHICKPEA OMELET FILLED WITH MUSHROOMS AND TOMATOES

Makes: *2 servings* | Time: *30 min*

This low-fat, gluten-free breakfast is for everyone who likes omelets but doesn't know how to veganize them. We use a juicy veggie filling in this recipe, but add whatever filling you crave for; the characteristic taste of chickpea flour mixed with kala namak will do the rest.

INGREDIENTS FOR FILLING

7 button mushrooms, sliced

1 scallion, sliced

5 cherry tomatoes, halved

¼ teaspoon salt

INGREDIENTS FOR OMELET

1 cup (125 g) chickpea flour

2 tablespoons tapioca starch

1 teaspoon kala namak (Himalayan black salt)

⅛ teaspoon turmeric powder

¾ cup (180 ml) unsweetened plant-based milk, e.g., rice milk

2 tablespoons cilantro, chopped

INSTRUCTIONS FOR FILLING

1. Heat a large nonstick pan to medium. Add the sliced mushrooms, scallions, and tomatoes. Sprinkle with the salt. Let everything cook until the mushrooms lose most of their water. Set aside.

INSTRUCTIONS FOR OMELET

1. In a bowl whisk together the chickpea flour, tapioca starch, kala namak, and turmeric powder. Add the plant-based milk and whisk until smooth. Add the chopped cilantro and whisk again.
2. Using a pan the same size as your plate, add oil or cooking spray and heat on medium-high. Pour half of the omelet batter into the pan for two small omelets or all the batter to make one big omelet. Tilt the pan until the batter spreads evenly across the bottom.
3. Cook the omelet for 3 to 4 minutes until the batter on the sides is set and the omelet is brown underneath, then flip and let it cook on the other side for 2 to 3 minutes.
4. Transfer the omelet onto the plate, add the filling, and fold it over. Enjoy!

CHOCOLATE CHIP PANCAKES

Makes: *5 pancakes* | Time: *30 min*

No egg replacements needed. These super-quick chocolate chip pancakes are the fluffiest ever. Plus, the chocolate chips give this breakfast treat a naughty bonus. Stack 'em, drizzle 'em, stuff 'em in your face. You deserve it.

INGREDIENTS

1 very ripe banana + a few extra slices for garnish

¾ cup (180 ml) unsweetened plant-based milk, e.g., rice milk

1 teaspoon maple syrup + extra for drizzling on top

1 teaspoon coconut oil

1 cup (125 g) all-purpose flour

1½ teaspoons baking powder

¼ cup (45 g) chocolate chips + a few more to add on top

INSTRUCTIONS

1. In a bowl, mash the peeled banana and add the plant-based milk, maple syrup, and coconut oil. Give it a quick whisk.
2. In a separate bowl, combine the flour and baking powder. Add in the wet ingredients. Whisk until incorporated. Fold in the chocolate chips. Let the batter sit for a few minutes.
3. Add oil to a flat or griddle pan and heat on medium to low. Add a small ladle of pancake batter. If the batter spreads too much in the pan, whisk a bit more flour into the mixture. If it doesn't spread enough, add a bit more plant-based milk. Let it cook until the middle becomes bubbly and the corners set, then flip with a spatula. Let it cook on the other side until done. Repeat for all pancakes.
4. Stack the pancakes, top with a few chocolate chips, and drizzle with maple syrup. Yay breakfast!

CHICKEN & WAFFLES

Makes: *2 servings (2 waffles and 3 chicken pieces each)* | Time: *90 min*

Did you ever crave sugary and salty at the same time? If you can't seem to decide between a sweet and savory breakfast, you'll be very happy with this chicken & waffles dish. In our recipe, we're using homemade waffles topped with fried seitan chicken nuggets, all drizzled with maple syrup. It's the perfect start to a lazy weekend.

INGREDIENTS FOR CHICKEN

½ cup (60 g) vital wheat gluten

¼ cup (30 g) chickpea flour + 1 cup (120 g), divided

½ tablespoon chicken seasoning* + ½ teaspoon, divided

⅓ cup (75 ml) sparkling water

1 cup (250 ml) water

¼ teaspoon sriracha

½ cup (75 g) breadcrumbs

¼ cup (40 g) all-purpose flour

¼ cup (15 g) panko flakes

oil for frying

INGREDIENTS FOR WAFFLES

1 cup (125 g) all-purpose flour

1½ teaspoons baking powder

2 tablespoons white sugar

¾ cup (180 ml) plant-based milk, e.g., rice milk

maple syrup, for topping

INSTRUCTIONS FOR CHICKEN

1. Combine vital wheat gluten, ¼ cup chickpea flour, and chicken seasoning in a mixing bowl. Add the sparkling water. Stir to combine and use a kitchen machine to knead the homemade seitan for 5 minutes or knead it by hand for 10 minutes.
2. Add a steaming basket to a large pot and fill with a couple of inches of water. Bring the water to a boil.
3. Divide the seitan into 6 equal pieces and press them into a nugget shape 1-inch (3 cm) thick. Add the seitan nuggets into the steaming basket and let them steam for about 20 minutes, flipping them after 10 minutes.
4. Combine the remaining chickpea flour, water, and sriracha and whisk until smooth.
5. In a separate bowl, combine the breadcrumbs, all-purpose flour, and panko flakes.
6. Once the nuggets are soft, let them cool off a bit, then dip them first in the egg replacement, then coat them in the breading. Repeat until all nuggets are coated.
7. Heat the oil for frying in a pot (just enough so that the nuggets can swim; make sure there's enough room in the pot to prevent it from spilling over) to 350°F/175°C, and carefully add the breaded seitan nuggets (work in batches). Fry for 4 minutes until golden and crispy and transfer the nuggets onto a paper towel to remove excess oil.

(Continued on next page)

---

*Make your own chicken seasoning by combining 1 teaspoon salt, ½ teaspoon paprika, ⅛ teaspoon pepper, and ⅛ teaspoon garlic powder.

INSTRUCTIONS FOR WAFFLES

1. Combine the flour, baking powder, and sugar in a mixing bowl. Add in the milk and whisk until combined. It should be a thick, sticky batter.
2. Heat a waffle iron and coat it generously with baking spray or coconut oil so that the waffles don't stick to the iron later.
3. Use about ¼ cup waffle batter for each waffle to make 4 waffles. Let the waffles cook in the iron or pan until slightly brown on the edges.
4. Once you've made all the waffles, stack them up, add the vegan chicken on top, and drizzle with maple syrup.

BREAKFAST WRAP

Makes: *3 medium-sized or 2 large wraps* | Time: *40 min*

This is breakfast you can hold in one hand. This breakfast wrap features a Mediterranean tofu scramble with green olives, sun-dried tomatoes, and homemade tempeh bacon. Don't want to use tempeh? Use tofu instead! Top with tomato and cucumber slices for added freshness.

INGREDIENTS FOR TEMPEH BACON

1½ tablespoons soy sauce

1½ tablespoons sesame oil

1 teaspoon liquid smoke

1 teaspoon maple syrup

⅛ teaspoon salt + more to taste

9 thin slices tempeh

INGREDIENTS FOR TOFU SCRAMBLE

10 oz. (280 g) firm tofu

1 teaspoon canola oil

¼ teaspoon turmeric powder

¼ teaspoon curry powder

¾ teaspoon kala namak (Himalayan black salt)

1 teaspoon dried oregano

1 teaspoon dried basil

1 tablespoon sun-dried tomatoes, chopped

2 tablespoons green olives, sliced

ADDITIONAL INGREDIENTS

3 wheat-flour tortillas

tomato slices

cucumber slices

INSTRUCTIONS FOR TEMPEH BACON

1. In a small bowl, whisk together the soy sauce, sesame oil, liquid smoke, maple syrup, and salt and pour it in a pan large enough to hold the sliced tempeh. Add in the tempeh slices in a single layer and let them soak in the marinade for 2 to 3 minutes, then flip them over and let them soak for another 2 minutes before bringing the pan to medium-high heat.
2. Cook the marinated tempeh slices for about 3 to 4 minutes (until lightly browned and crispy), then flip and let them cook on the other side for 2 to 3 minutes as well. Set aside.

INSTRUCTIONS FOR TOFU SCRAMBLE

1. Scramble the tofu with your hands or a fork.
2. Heat the canola oil in a large pan and add in scrambled tofu.
3. Add the turmeric powder, curry powder, and kala namak. Mix well until the tofu takes on an even yellow color. Keep it on medium to high heat while stirring for about 7 minutes. Add the oregano, basil, sun-dried tomatoes, and green olives. Give the scramble a stir and let it cook for another 2 minutes until warm. Add more kala namak to taste.

TO ASSEMBLE

1. In a pan, heat the tortillas until warm. Divide the tofu scramble onto the three tortillas, top with three slices of tempeh bacon each, and add tomato and cucumber slices. Fold the wrap and enjoy!

FRUITY GRANOLA

Makes: *1½ cups* | Time: *20 min*

With only 5 ingredients and 20 minutes to prepare, this fruity granola with strawberries and raspberries is the way to go when you're craving a quick, delicious, and healthy breakfast. Swap out fruits or add chocolate and even tiny vegan marshmallows if you like. Enjoy with milk, yogurt, or if you're feeling naughty, on ice cream. There's really no limit to this versatile recipe.

INGREDIENTS

⅓ cup (10 g) freeze-dried strawberries

⅛ cup (10 g) freeze-dried raspberries

2 tablespoons white almond butter

2 tablespoons maple syrup

1 cup (90 g) rolled oats*

INSTRUCTIONS

1. Preheat the oven to 360°F/180°C.
2. Chop the freeze-dried strawberries and raspberries into small bits.
3. In a mixing bowl, add the almond butter and maple syrup and give it a mix. Add in the rolled oats and chopped fruit and mix again until clumpy.
4. Place the mixture on a baking sheet lined with parchment paper and spread it until it's about 1-inch thick.
5. Bake the granola in the oven for about 10 to 15 minutes while tossing it around every 3 minutes to allow even baking without burning bits. Let the granola cool off before breaking it into chunks. Eat it with vegan milk, yogurt, or on ice cream. Keep this granola in an airtight jar and store at room temperature for up to six months. Enjoy!

---

*To make this recipe gluten free, make sure you use certified gluten-free oats.

CHOCOLATE WAFFLES WITH PEANUT BUTTER

Makes: *7 small waffles* | Time: *30 min*

If you're looking for a decadent breakfast or brunch idea, you can't go wrong with these chocolate waffles drizzled with peanut butter and sprinkled with shaved chocolate. If you want to mix things up, use maple syrup or almond butter instead of peanut butter, or top the waffles with fresh berries or jam! Whatever you do, it's a hell of a naughty way to start your day.

INGREDIENTS FOR WAFFLES

1 cup (120 g) all-purpose flour

1 teaspoon baking powder

1 pinch salt

2 tablespoons cocoa powder

1 tablespoon maple syrup

¾ cup (180 ml) unsweetened plant-based milk

ADDITIONAL INGREDIENTS

2 tablespoons peanut butter

optional: ¼ cup (60 ml) hot water or more until the peanut butter sauce is drizzly*

1 teaspoon maple syrup

1 oz. (15g) dairy-free chocolate

INSTRUCTIONS FOR WAFFLES

1. Preheat the waffle iron.
2. Add the flour, baking powder, salt, and cocoa powder in a mixing bowl and give it a quick whisk. Add the maple syrup and plant-based milk. Whisk until incorporated. Let the mixture sit for a few minutes.
3. Meanwhile, prepare the peanut butter sauce. In a separate bowl, whisk the peanut butter, hot water (if needed), and maple syrup until it's perfectly drizzly.
4. Use a veggie peeler to shave the chocolate.
5. Once the waffle iron is hot, spray it with nonstick cooking spray and add about an ice cream scoop-sized amount of batter for each waffle. Cook waffles in the iron until steam stops coming out of the iron and the waffle edges are slightly brown.
6. Once you've made all the waffles, drizzle with the peanut butter sauce and top with shaved chocolate. Best start to the day ever.

---

*If you store your peanut butter at room temperature, you may require less or no water to get a drizzly peanut-butter consistency!

DILL & CAPER ALMOND CREAM CHEESE

Makes: *½ cup* | Time: *10 min + soaking overnight*

See how short this recipe is? That's because it's easy as hell. This simple almond cream cheese is perfect for bagels. Hate capers or dill? Try adding parsley or chives for an herb-filled twist. Feeling adventurous? Leave out the salt and try a sweet version with brown sugar and fresh berries.

INGREDIENTS

½ cup (75 g) blanched almonds (soaked overnight; see instructions)

2 teaspoons lemon juice

3 tablespoons water

¼ teaspoon salt

1 tablespoon capers

2 tablespoons dill, chopped

INSTRUCTIONS

1. Soak the blanched almonds in water overnight. Rinse and drain.
2. Place all ingredients in a food processor and pulse until creamy.
3. Transfer the cream cheese to a bowl and let it chill in the fridge for at least 1 hour to thicken, then smear it on your bagel or bread of choice! Store cream cheese in an airtight container in your fridge for up to 3 days.

CREAMY EGG SPREAD

Makes: *½ cup* | Time: *5 min*

Simple yet amazing. If you have a desire for egg salad, this no-egg spread will be the perfect way to tackle your craving headfirst. While the silken tofu provides an ideal consistency and texture, the kala namak, or Himalayan black salt, adds a typical eggy flavor. Yum.

INGREDIENTS

½ cup (150 g) silken tofu

½ teaspoon kala namak (Himalayan black salt) + more to taste

¼ teaspoon curry powder

⅛ teaspoon turmeric powder

pinch black pepper + more to sprinkle on top

2 teaspoons fresh chives, chopped + more to sprinkle on top

INSTRUCTIONS

1. Place the silken tofu in a bowl and use a fork to mash it into smaller pieces.
2. Add the rest of the ingredients to the bowl and give it a good mix. Add more kala namak to taste.
3. Spread over bread slices or in a bowl by itself and sprinkle with more black pepper and chives. To store it, keep this spread in an airtight jar and store it in the fridge for 1 to 2 days.

BREAKFAST PIZZA

Makes: *1 large pizza for 2 people* | Time: *1 hour + 2 hours rising time*

Yes, it's pizza for breakfast. Or breakfast for dinner? Either way, this is the ultimate vegan breakfast pizza with tofu scramble and homemade seitan sausages! If you have enough time and motivation, you can make the crust, vegan cheese, and seitan sausage from scratch. If you don't, using your favorite store-bought items will provide an excellent shortcut.

INGREDIENTS FOR PIZZA DOUGH

1¾ cups all-purpose flour
¼ teaspoon salt
½ teaspoon instant yeast
½ cup warm water
1 teaspoon olive oil

INGREDIENTS FOR TOFU SCRAMBLE

1¼ cups firm tofu
1 teaspoon canola oil
½ teaspoon curry powder
¼ teaspoon turmeric powder
1 teaspoon kala namak (Himalayan black salt)

ADDITIONAL INGREDIENTS

1 seitan sausage, sliced or sausages from our hot dog recipe (pg. 35)
¼ cup tomato passata*
½ teaspoon dried oregano + more for sprinkling on top
⅛ teaspoon salt
⅓ cup vegan cheese, shredded or cheese sauce from our loaded nachos recipe (pg. 83)

INSTRUCTIONS FOR PIZZA DOUGH

1. Put all dry ingredients in a kitchen machine or mix by hand, then add in the wet ingredients. Stir to combine, then knead until a smooth dough forms. Add more water if mixture is too crumbly; add more flour if it's too sticky. Cover the dough with a clean kitchen towel and let it rise until it doubles in size.

INSTRUCTIONS FOR TOFU SCRAMBLE

1. Scramble the tofu with your hands or a fork.
2. Heat the canola oil in a large pan and add in scrambled tofu.
3. Add the curry powder, turmeric, and kala namak. Mix well until the tofu takes on an even yellow color. Keep it on medium to high heat while stirring for about 5 minutes. Add more kala namak to taste.
4. Preheat the oven to 480°F/250°C.
5. Roll out the dough until it forms a nice pizza base and put it on a baking tray lined with parchment paper. Set aside.
6. Mix the tomato passata with the dried oregano and salt and spread it evenly over the pizza base. Add the vegan cheese over the pizza sauce. Add the tofu scramble onto the pizza and top with sliced seitan sausage.
7. Bake the pizza in the oven for about 10 to 15 minutes. The pizza is ready when it has a golden crust. Sprinkle with oregano after baking and enjoy!

---

*I used store-bought tomato passata (with salt, no additional herbs) for this recipe. It's often canned or in cartons; not to confuse with tomato paste, which is thicker in consistency.

A LETTER OF REJECTION TO LUNCH SALADS

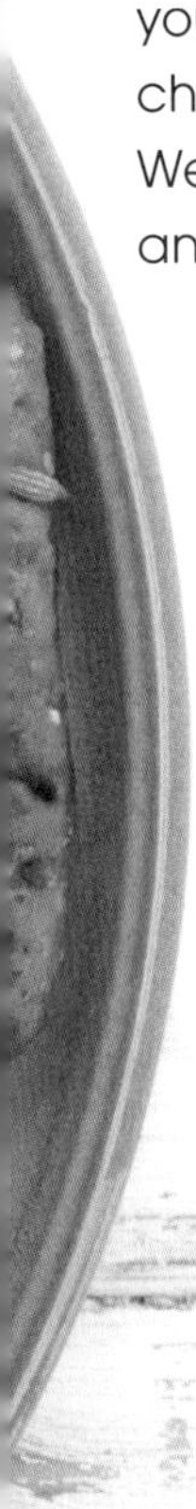

Let me guess, the smart and unhungry version of you from yesterday bought a pre-packaged salad for lunch again. *Ugh.* While having a light lunch is one of the best ways to stay productive during the day, sometimes a bunch of leaves topped with oil and vinegar just doesn't cut it. So, how do you treat-yo-self after or during a crappy day? Maybe you've tried your own vegan meat and cheese alternatives but making seitan from scratch seems like a chore, and you don't even know where to start with vegan cheese. We've got you covered! We've made quesadillas, seitan shawarma, mac & cheese, fried chicken burgers, hot dogs, and so much more. This is how you make them yourself.

HOT DOGS

Makes: *4 hot dogs* | Time: *90 min*

With our recipe for homemade Seitan Sausages, you can take this classic ballpark snack to the next level. We've topped our hot dogs very traditionally with ketchup, pickles, and fried onions, but feel free to experiment with more adventurous toppings such as guacamole, salsa, or chili sin carne.

INGREDIENTS FOR SEITAN SAUSAGES

½ tablespoon canola oil

½ large white onion, chopped

1 garlic clove, chopped

½ teaspoon cumin seeds

½ teaspoon fennel seeds

¼ cup (40 g) chickpeas

1 tablespoon tomato paste

⅛ teaspoon salt

½ teaspoon thyme

½ teaspoon smoked paprika

1 tablespoon soy sauce

¼ cup (60 ml) sparkling water

¾ cup (90 g) vital wheat gluten

ADDITIONAL INGREDIENTS

4 hot dog buns

ketchup

pickles

fried onions

INSTRUCTIONS FOR SEITAN SAUSAGES

1. In a large pan with canola oil, sauté the chopped onion and garlic until soft. Add the cumin and fennel seeds. Cook until the spices are toasted.
2. In a food processor, add the chickpeas, onion-garlic-spice mixture, tomato paste, salt, thyme, smoked paprika, soy sauce, and sparkling water. Pulse until saucy, then add the vital wheat gluten and pulse again until mixture comes together in a ball.
3. Add a steaming basket to a large pot and fill with a couple of inches of water. Bring the water to a boil.
4. Divide the seitan into 4 equal chunks. Roll and press the seitan into a sausage shape. Roll each sausage in parchment paper and aluminum foil. Twist the ends so that the seitan is completely closed off. Add the seitan sausages into the steaming basket and let them steam for about 40 minutes, flipping them after 20 minutes.
5. Let them cool off a bit before removing the aluminum foil and parchment paper. Heat the sausages in a grill pan or contact grill for nice grill marks, then add them to your hot dog buns and top with ketchup, pickles, and fried onions. Serve with a side of french fries* and enjoy!

*For quick and easy fries, wash potatoes, cut them in equally large fry-shaped pieces, toss in olive oil, salt, and pepper and transfer them on a baking tray lined with parchment paper. Bake at 400°F/200°C until golden and crispy.

MUSHROOM BURGER

Makes: *6 burgers* | Time: *1 hour*

For this recipe, we didn't just grill a portobello and call it a burger (not that there's anything wrong with that). No, this is an actual burger patty using the awesome texture of freshly roasted button mushrooms. Unlike many vegan burger recipes, these homemade mushroom patties will not fall apart. Serve with caramelized red onions, mango chutney, and fresh arugula in a pretzel bun. Perfect.

INGREDIENTS FOR MUSHROOM PATTIES

1 lb. (500 g) fresh button mushrooms, halved

1 red onion

½ cup (70 g) raw sunflower seeds

½ cup (50 g) rolled oats

¼ cup (25 g) breadcrumbs

¼ cup (10 g) fresh dill

¼ teaspoon salt

canola oil for brushing the tops

ADDITIONAL INGREDIENTS

6 pretzel buns

1 cup (20 g) arugula

¼ cup (85 g) mango chutney

INSTRUCTIONS FOR MUSHROOM PATTIES

1. Preheat the oven to 400°F/200°C.
2. Clean the mushrooms, then cook them in a pan without oil on medium to high heat until they are soft. Set aside and let them cool off a bit.
3. Peel and cut the red onion into rings. Slowly caramelize the red onion in a pan while adding bits of water when the rings start to stick to the bottom.
4. Transfer the cooked mushrooms and about ⅓ of the caramelized onions to the food processor. Add sunflower seeds, oats, breadcrumbs, fresh dill, and salt. Process until combined. You should be able to form 6 patties. If the mixture is too crumbly, add tiny splashes of water; if it's too sticky, add more breadcrumbs.
5. Place the mushroom patties on a baking tray lined with parchment paper. Spray or brush the patties with the canola oil and bake them in the oven for 20 to 25 minutes, flipping them once halfway through. They should be slightly browned. Store patties in the freezer for up to 1 month by layering them between small sheets of parchment paper to prevent them from sticking together. Let them thaw after taking them out of the freezer and reheat in a pan with a little bit of oil.

TO ASSEMBLE

1. Slice the pretzel buns open, add fresh arugula, the mushroom patty, spread mango chutney on top, and add the remaining caramelized onions.

SPICY STOVETOP MAC & CHEESE

Makes: *2 servings* | Time: *50 min*

Nothing screams comfort food more than mac & cheese. Its savory creaminess was something we've been trying to recreate forever, until one day Bianca added tapioca starch to the sauce and a choir of cheesy angels sang its song of ethereal divinity and excitedly exclaimed, "Hallelujah, for this is the best cheese sauce to ever touch our heavenly angel tongues." Or something like that. As a main or side dish, with or without the spiciness, we could eat this forever. And we probably will.

INGREDIENTS FOR VEGAN CHEESE SAUCE

2 tablespoons coconut oil or vegan butter

½ teaspoon salt

¼ teaspoon curry powder

¼ teaspoon paprika powder

ground pepper to taste

⅓ cup (40 g) all-purpose flour

1 tablespoon tapioca starch

⅓ cup (15 g) nutritional yeast

½ cup (120 g) water

½ teaspoon sriracha + more to taste

ADDITIONAL INGREDIENTS

2 servings cooked macaroni pasta + reserved pasta water (to thin out the cheese sauce)

cayenne pepper

2 teaspoons fresh chives

INSTRUCTIONS FOR VEGAN CHEESE SAUCE

1. Heat the coconut oil or butter in a small pot over low heat.
2. Add the salt, curry powder, paprika powder, and pepper.
3. Add in the flour and tapioca starch and whisk.
4. Add in nutritional yeast and whisk again until clumpy.
5. Add the water and whisk on low heat for a few minutes until it gets gooey, then add in the sriracha to taste. If the cheese gets too thick, add a little bit more water to thin it out and whisk again. Set aside.
6. Combine the cooked pasta and cheese sauce (use the saved pasta water to thin out the sauce).
7. Plate the mac and cheese and sprinkle it with cayenne pepper and chopped chives. Enjoy, then get back to cooking because you are going to want more!

PHILLY CHEESESTEAK

Makes: *2 Philly cheesesteaks* | Time: *90 min*

You'd be surprised how easy it is to recreate a classic Philly cheesesteak with all-vegan ingredients. The most important trick to getting this recipe right is making sure that when you take that first bite, the juice pours out of your sandwich and onto everything. If you're finishing this with a clean shirt, you've clearly done something wrong.

INGREDIENTS FOR SEITAN

½ tablespoon canola oil

½ large white onion, chopped

1 garlic clove, chopped

½ teaspoon cumin seeds

½ teaspoon fennel seeds

¼ cup (40 g) chickpeas

1 tablespoon tomato paste

⅛ teaspoon salt

½ teaspoon thyme

½ teaspoon smoked paprika

1 tablespoon soy sauce

¼ cup (60 ml) sparkling water

¾ cup (90 g) vital wheat gluten

INGREDIENTS FOR CHEESE SAUCE

2 tablespoons coconut oil or vegan butter

½ teaspoon salt

⅛ teaspoon turmeric powder

¼ teaspoon curry powder

¼ teaspoon paprika powder

⅓ cup (40 g) all-purpose flour

⅓ cup (15 g) nutritional yeast

½ cup (120 g) water

INSTRUCTIONS FOR SEITAN

1. In a large pan with canola oil, sauté the chopped onion and garlic until soft. Add the cumin and fennel seeds and cook until the spices are toasted.
2. In a food processor, add the chickpeas, onion-garlic-spice mixture, tomato paste, salt, thyme, smoked paprika, soy sauce, and sparkling water. Pulse until saucy, then add the vital wheat gluten and pulse again until it comes together in a ball.
3. Add a steaming basket to a large pot and fill with a couple of inches of water. Bring the water to a boil.
4. Divide the seitan into 8 equal chunks. Add the seitan chunks into the steaming basket and let them steam for about 40 minutes, flipping them after 20 minutes.

INSTRUCTIONS FOR CHEESE SAUCE

1. Heat the coconut oil or butter in a small pot over low heat.
2. Add the salt, turmeric powder, curry powder, and paprika powder.
3. Add in the flour and whisk.
4. Add in nutritional yeast and whisk again until clumpy.
5. Add in the water and whisk on low heat for 1 to 2 minutes until the sauce gets gooey. Set aside. If the sauce gets too thick later on, add a little bit more water to thin it out and whisk again.

(Continued on next page)

ADDITIONAL INGREDIENTS

1 white onion, peeled, halved, and sliced

¼ green bell pepper, cut into strips

¼ red bell pepper, cut into strips

2 sandwich buns

TO ASSEMBLE

1. Let the seitan cool off a bit before slicing it into thin strips.
2. Bring a large pan with olive oil to high heat, toss in the white onion, and let it cook until translucent. Add in the bell pepper and seitan strips and let it pan-fry for 3 to 4 minutes until the seitan is crispy on the edges and the bell pepper is softened. Add more salt to taste.
3. Fill the sandwich buns with crispy seitan and top with the cheese sauce. Enjoy!

MARGHERITA PIZZA WITH CASHEW MOZZARELLA

Makes: *2 pizzas* | Time: *70 min + soaking overnight + 1 hour cooling time for cashew mozzarella*

While we usually don't give too many you-know-whats about authenticity, there's a case to make for a classic, minimalistic Margherita pizza. While the crust is great, the true star of this recipe is the homemade cashew mozzarella that will make you stop thinking about its dairy counterpart. Plus, it's way easier to make than you might think! Add all the toppings you like, but make sure to give this cashew mozzarella the spotlight it deserves.

INGREDIENTS FOR CASHEW MOZZARELLA*

1 cup (130 g) raw, unsalted cashews (soaked overnight; see instructions)

4 teaspoons tapioca starch

2 small garlic cloves

4 tablespoons nutritional yeast

¾ teaspoon salt

2 teaspoons lemon juice

½ cup (125 ml) water

INGREDIENTS FOR PIZZA CRUST

2½ cups (300 g) all-purpose flour

1 teaspoon instant yeast

½ teaspoon salt

1 teaspoon olive oil

¾ cup (180 ml) lukewarm water, divided

INSTRUCTIONS FOR CASHEW MOZZARELLA

1. Soak the cashews in water overnight. The next day, rinse and drain the cashews.
2. Place all the cashew mozzarella ingredients in a blender and blend until completely smooth. You might have to scrape down the sides a few times.
3. Transfer the cheese mixture into a saucepan and bring to medium heat. Keep stirring until it gets stretchy and comes together in a ball. Then, transfer the cheese ball into a container, let it cool off, close the lid, and let it chill in the fridge for at least 1 hour.
4. Slice the cashew mozzarella and use it on this pizza, in quesadillas, in grilled cheese sandwiches, or however you would use regular mozzarella!

INSTRUCTIONS FOR PIZZA CRUST

1. Add the flour, instant yeast, and salt in a large mixing bowl and stir to combine.
2. Add in the oil and water. Combine all ingredients with a large spoon, then knead by hand or put all the

(Continued on next page)

*You won't need all the vegan cheese you make for this recipe, but I've doubled the ingredients to make it work in a regular blender as well. If you're using a blender with a small container, feel free to halve the cheese recipe. If you plan on making this cheese but don't know when exactly, you can keep the cashews soaking in water in the fridge for a few months. You can keep the mozzarella in an airtight container in the fridge for 2 to 3 days.

INGREDIENTS FOR SAUCE

½ cup (110 g) tomato passata
dried basil to taste
dried oregano to taste
salt to taste
garlic powder to taste
cracked black pepper
fresh basil (about 10 leaves)

ingredients in a bread baking machine and let the machine knead the dough until a soft dough forms.

3. Cover the bowl of dough with a clean kitchen towel in a warm spot and let it sit for 1½ to 2 hours until the dough doubles in size.
4. Preheat the oven to 480°F/250°C.
5. Add more flour to the dough and work it into the mixture until it's smooth and nonstick. Divide the dough and roll it out to two pizza crusts on lightly floured parchment paper.

INSTRUCTIONS FOR SAUCE

1. Mix the tomato passata with the dried basil, dried oregano, salt, and garlic powder to taste. Spread it onto the pizza crusts.

TO ASSEMBLE

1. Add slices of the mozzarella, and sprinkle with cracked black pepper.
2. Bake the pizzas in the oven for about 10 to 15 minutes, until the crust is golden and the tomato sauce has thickened.
3. Sprinkle with fresh basil leaves before serving!

WALNUT MEAT TACOS

Makes: *8 tacos* | Time: *25 min*

This one surprised us. Did you know you can make a delicious ground meat alternative out of walnuts? The crumbly texture makes for an unexpectedly excellent alternative to use in tacos, burritos, or on salads. You can also sprinkle it over your favorite pasta dish to add that extra crunch.

INGREDIENTS FOR WALNUT MEAT

1 red onion, peeled, halved

1 garlic clove, peeled

1 teaspoon olive oil

1 cup (100 g) walnuts (raw, no shell, unsalted)

½ teaspoon soy sauce

¼ teaspoon paprika powder

¼ teaspoon salt

¼ teaspoon dried thyme

ADDITIONAL INGREDIENTS

8 taco shells*

2 cups (40 g) mixed greens

½ cup (30 g) shredded purple cabbage

3 tablespoons canned corn, rinsed and drained

8 cherry tomatoes, halved

1 tablespoon vegan mayo**

2 tablespoons cilantro, chopped

INSTRUCTIONS FOR WALNUT MEAT

1. In a food processor, chop the red onion and garlic clove to your liking. In a pan, add the olive oil and bring to medium-high heat. Add the chopped onion and garlic and cook until softened and translucent.
2. Chop the walnuts in a food processor until coarsely ground. Add them to the onion and garlic mixture in the pan. Mix in the soy sauce, paprika powder, salt, and thyme. Combine everything and cook for 5 to 7 minutes while stirring a few times to prevent burning, until nice and toasty. Add more salt or soy sauce to taste.

TO ASSEMBLE

1. Add onto each taco mixed greens, purple cabbage, canned corn, cherry tomatoes, and the walnut meat. Drizzle the tacos with the vegan mayo and sprinkle with chopped cilantro. Enjoy!

---

*There's a simple trick how to make your own hard-shell tacos if you only have soft tortillas at home. Fold the soft tortillas over your oven rack. Let them bake for about 5 to 8 minutes at 350°F/180°C. They should be nice and crispy!

**To make a quick vegan mayo, to a bowl add ⅛ cup (30 ml) unsweetened soy milk, ¼ teaspoon apple cider vinegar, ⅛ teaspoon mustard, ⅛ teaspoon maple syrup, ¼ teaspoon salt, and ½ teaspoon lime juice. With an immersion blender mix for 1 minute then slowly drizzle ⅓ cup (80 g) canola oil while the immersion blender is running. Blend 3 minutes until the mayo is thick and creamy. Add more salt, mustard, or lime juice to taste. Store in the fridge for up to 3 days. Add a splash of water to make the mayo easier to drizzle.

SPAGHETTI CARBONARA

Makes: *2 servings* | Time: *30 min*

They say you shouldn't put any cream or milk in your carbonara, and we agree, but nobody said anything about plant-based milk. (Actually, we're sure that many people have said exactly that—many times.) By using smoky tofu bits as the main meat alternative and creating a sauce from silken tofu flavored with nutritional yeast (for a cheesy component) and kala namak (for an eggy flavor) we tried a risky take on spaghetti carbonara, and it worked. To hell with authenticity, it's delicious!

INGREDIENTS FOR SMOKY TOFU BITS

4 oz. (110 g) firm tofu

1 tablespoon canola oil

¼ teaspoon paprika powder

½ teaspoon liquid smoke

1 teaspoon soy sauce

INGREDIENTS FOR SPAGHETTI CARBONARA

8 oz. (250 g) silken tofu

4 tablespoons nutritional yeast

1½ teaspoons kala namak (Himalayan black salt)

1 dash curry powder

lime juice from 1 lime

½ cup (125 ml) unsweetened plant-based milk (e.g., rice milk)

¼ teaspoon salt + more to taste

cooked spaghetti for 2 (save the cooking water to thin out the sauce)

cracked black pepper

1 teaspoon parsley, chopped

INSTRUCTIONS FOR SMOKY TOFU BITS

1. Cut the tofu into small bits. Add the canola oil to a large pan and heat to medium. Add in the tofu, then the paprika powder, liquid smoke, and soy sauce. Give it a quick stir and close the pan with a lid. Stir the tofu around every couple of minutes. Fry the tofu until crispy on all sides for 5 to 7 minutes. Transfer the tofu bits onto paper towels to remove excess oil and set aside.

INSTRUCTIONS FOR SPAGHETTI CARBONARA

1. Put the silken tofu, nutritional yeast, kala namak, curry powder, lime juice, plant-based milk, and salt in a blender and blend until completely smooth. You might have to scrape down the sides.
2. Place the drained spaghetti in a large pot and add in the carbonara sauce. Heat until warm and use the cooking water from the pasta to thin out the sauce until it has reached a consistency to your liking.
3. Plate the spaghetti carbonara, add the smoky tofu bits on top, and sprinkle with cracked black pepper and chopped parsley.

RED BEET BURGER

Makes: *3 patties* | Time: *25 min + 30 minutes chill time*

This amazing red beet burger is made out of protein-rich soy granule for a meaty texture. The red beet juice gives it a lovely pink color. Put it in whatever bun you have handy, grab your favorite condiments, and fire up your pans and grills, because this is the burger you've been waiting for.

INGREDIENTS FOR BURGER PATTIES

1 cup (60 g) soy granule

½ cup (120 ml) hot water

2 tablespoons red beet juice

¾ teaspoon salt

¼ teaspoon thyme

⅛ teaspoon garlic powder

¼ cup oat flour

2 teaspoons canola oil

ADDITIONAL INGREDIENTS

pretzel buns

lettuce

vegan mayo*

INSTRUCTIONS FOR BURGER PATTIES

1. Add the soy granule to a bowl, then add in the hot water and red beet juice and let the granule soak for 3 to 4 minutes until soft. Add the salt, thyme, and garlic powder and give it a mix. Then, add the oat flour and stir to combine.
2. Divide the mixture into three parts; form balls first, then press them into a patty shape. Add in more oat flour if the patties don't stick together.
3. Let the patties chill in the fridge for at least 30 minutes.
4. Heat a pan with the canola oil and pan-fry the patties on each side for 3 to 4 minutes on medium-high heat until golden and crispy.

TO ASSEMBLE

1. Serve in pretzel buns with lettuce and vegan mayo.

*To make a quick vegan mayo, to a bowl add ⅛ cup (30 ml) unsweetened soy milk, ¼ teaspoon apple cider vinegar, ⅛ teaspoon mustard, ⅛ teaspoon maple syrup, ¼ teaspoon salt, and ½ teaspoon lime juice. With an immersion blender mix for 1 minute then slowly drizzle ⅓ cup (80 g) canola oil while the immersion blender is running. Blend 3 minutes until the mayo is thick and creamy. Add more salt, mustard, or lime juice to taste. Store in the fridge for up to 3 days. Add a splash of water to make the mayo easier to drizzle.

QUESADILLAS WITH CASHEW CHEESE

Makes: *2 quesadillas* | Time: *40 min + soaking overnight*

Melted cheese between two tortillas; how can you go wrong? A quesadilla is a simple, delicious meal that will get you through those sad days or nasty hangovers. For the cheesy component of the quesadilla, we use our homemade cashew cheese. For the fillings, we use a mix of veggies such as red bell pepper, scallions, garlic, and corn, but you can use whatever you have at home. Just make sure you cook the fillings first to make them nice and soft for the quesadilla.

INGREDIENTS FOR CASHEW CHEESE*

1 cup (130 g) raw, unsalted cashews (soaked overnight; see instructions)

4 teaspoons tapioca starch

2 small garlic cloves

4 tablespoons nutritional yeast

¾ teaspoon salt

2 teaspoons lemon juice

½ cup (125 ml) water

INGREDIENTS FOR FILLING

1 teaspoon canola oil

1 red bell pepper, diced

1 scallion, thinly sliced

1 garlic clove, minced

½ cup (85 g) corn

½ teaspoon salt

¼ teaspoon cumin

cayenne pepper to taste

1 teaspoon cilantro, chopped

4 (9-inch) tortillas

INSTRUCTIONS FOR CASHEW CHEESE

1. Soak the cashews in water overnight. The next day, rinse and drain the cashews.
2. Place all the ingredients in a blender and blend until completely smooth. You might have to scrape down the sides a few times.
3. Transfer the cheese mixture into a saucepan and bring to medium heat. Keep stirring until it gets stretchy. Set aside.

INSTRUCTIONS FOR FILLING

1. Heat the canola oil in a large pan over high heat. Add the chopped veggies and season with salt, cumin, and cayenne pepper. Once the vegetables are soft, add the chopped cilantro and combine.
2. Spread the cashew cheese onto four tortillas all the way to the sides. Add the roasted veggies on two of the cheesy tortillas. Top each tortilla with a second cheesy tortilla and press them together until the filling sticks to the tortillas (thanks to the cheese).
3. Bake each quesadilla in a lightly oiled pan for 2 to 3 minutes until crispy, then flip and bake on the other side until golden and crispy. Cut into quarters and serve.

*You won't need all the vegan cheese for this recipe, but I've doubled the ingredients to make it work in a regular blender as well. If you're using a blender with a small container, feel free to halve the cheese recipe.

SHAWARMA

Makes: *4 servings* | Time: *95 min*

Shawarma is one of the most universally popular street foods. Our version includes homemade seitan and is served in thick and fluffy tortillas with lettuce, cucumber, tomatoes, and yogurt sauce. Awesome.

INGREDIENTS FOR SEITAN

1 tablespoon canola oil

1 large white onion, chopped

2 garlic cloves, chopped

1 teaspoon cumin seeds

1 teaspoon fennel seeds

½ cup (85 g) chickpeas

2 tablespoons tomato paste

¼ teaspoon salt

1 teaspoon thyme

1 teaspoon smoked paprika

2 tablespoons soy sauce

½ cup (120 ml) sparkling water

1½ cups (180 g) vital wheat gluten

INGREDIENTS FOR FLUFFY TORTILLAS

3⅓ cups (400 g) all-purpose flour

2 teaspoons baking powder

½ teaspoon salt

1 tablespoon olive oil

1 cup (250 g) water

INGREDIENTS FOR YOGURT SAUCE

¼ cup (100 g) unsweetened soy yogurt

INSTRUCTIONS FOR SEITAN

1. In a large pan with canola oil, sauté the chopped onion and garlic cloves until soft. Add in the cumin and fennel seeds and cook further until the seeds are toasted.
2. In a food processor, add the chickpeas, onion-garlic-spice mixture, tomato paste, salt, thyme, smoked paprika, soy sauce, and sparkling water. Pulse until it's saucy, then add the vital wheat gluten and pulse again until it comes together in a ball.
3. Add a steaming basket to a large pot and fill with a couple of inches of water. Bring the water to a boil.
4. Divide the seitan into 8 equal chunks. Add the seitan chunks into the steaming basket and let them steam for about 40 minutes, flipping them after 20 minutes.
5. Let the seitan cool off a bit before slicing it into thin strips.
6. Bring a large pan with olive oil to high heat, toss in the seitan strips, and pan-fry them for 3 to 4 minutes or until crispy around the edges.

INSTRUCTIONS FOR FLUFFY TORTILLAS

1. In a mixing bowl add the dry ingredients first and give it a mix, then pour in the oil and add the water little by little. Stir to combine and knead with your hands until a smooth dough forms. Add more water if the mixture is too crumbly; add more flour if it's too sticky.

(Continued on next page)

⅛ teaspoon salt

1 drizzle olive oil

1 teaspoon chives, chopped

½ teaspoon lime juice

ADDITIONAL INGREDIENTS

8 leaves of lettuce

¼ cucumber, sliced and halved

1 tomato, sliced and halved

chives for topping

2. Divide the dough into 4 equal pieces, then shape the pieces into balls and roll them out on a floured surface.
3. Put one tortilla in a very hot (!) nonstick pan (a flat pan like a crepe-pan works best) and let it cook for up to 1 minute until it starts getting bubbly on the surface. Then, flip the tortilla to cook the other side. Repeat for the other tortillas.
4. Keep the tortillas covered in a clean kitchen towel until serving to keep them soft and flexible.

INSTRUCTIONS FOR YOGURT SAUCE

1. Whisk together all ingredients.

TO ASSEMBLE

1. On each tortilla, add 2 lettuce leaves and the seitan shawarma. Top with cucumber slices, tomato slices, and the yogurt sauce. Sprinkle with more fresh chives. Fold the tortilla and enjoy!

FRIED CHICKEN BURGER

Makes: *2 servings* | Time: *65 min*

If you ate chicken in the past, you must have craved this dish at least once since you've made the switch to veganism. Our take on a classic fried chicken burger includes homemade seitan, breaded and fried until golden brown and crispy. It's perfect. Add some lettuce and vegan mayo, and you're already good to go. You can also add tomatoes, pickles, mustard, BBQ sauce, hot sauce, or whatever your heart (or stomach) desires.

INGREDIENTS FOR CHICKEN PATTIES

½ cup (60 g) vital wheat gluten

¼ cup (30 g) + 1 cup chickpea flour, divided

½ tablespoon + ½ teaspoon chicken seasoning*

⅓ cup (75 ml) sparkling water

oil for frying

1 cup (250 ml) water

¼ teaspoon sriracha

½ cup (75 g) breadcrumbs

¼ cup (40 g) all-purpose flour

¼ cup (15 g) panko flakes

ADDITIONAL INGREDIENTS

2 burger buns

lettuce, chopped

vegan mayo*

INSTRUCTIONS FOR CHICKEN PATTIES

1. Combine vital wheat gluten, ¼ cup chickpea flour, and ½ tablespoon chicken seasoning for the seitan chicken in a mixing bowl. Add the sparkling water. Stir to combine and let the kitchen machine knead the seitan for 5 minutes or knead it by hand for 10 minutes.
2. Add a steaming basket to a large pot and fill with a couple of inches of water. Bring the water to a boil.
3. Divide the seitan into 2 equal pieces and press each piece into a chicken filet shape about 1-inch (3 cm) thick. Add the seitan to the steaming basket and let it steam for about 20 minutes, flipping it after 10 minutes.
4. In a bowl combine the remaining chickpea flour, water, and sriracha sauce for the egg replacement and whisk until smooth.
5. In a separate bowl combine the breadcrumbs, all-purpose flour, panko flakes, and remaining chicken seasoning.
6. Once the steamed seitan chicken filets are soft and cooled off, dip them first in the egg replacement, then coat them in the breading.

(Continued on next page)

*To make a quick vegan mayo, to a bowl add ⅛ cup (30 ml) unsweetened soy milk, ¼ teaspoon apple cider vinegar, ⅛ teaspoon mustard, ⅛ teaspoon maple syrup, ¼ teaspoon salt, and ½ teaspoon lime juice. With an immersion blender mix for 1 minute then slowly drizzle ⅓ cup (80 g) canola oil while the immersion blender is running. Blend 3 minutes until the mayo is thick and creamy. Add more salt, mustard, or lime juice to taste. Store in the fridge for up to 3 days. Add a splash of water to make the mayo easier to drizzle.

7. Heat the frying oil in a pot (just enough so that the chicken patties can swim; make sure there's enough room in the pot to prevent it from spilling over) to 350°F/175°C, and carefully add the breaded seitan filets (work in batches). Let each patty fry for about 4 minutes until golden and crispy. Transfer each seitan patty onto a paper towel to remove excess oil.

TO ASSEMBLE

1. Add chicken patties to the burger buns. Top each patty with chopped lettuce and any other toppings you desire. Spread vegan mayo onto the top burger buns and enjoy!

CRAB CAKES

Makes: *5 crab cakes* | Time: *20 min*

Whether you love them or hate them, if you take kindly to seafood-inspired vegan treats, give these crab cakes a shot. We've added all the typical ingredients for a fishy flavor: nori, dill, lemon juice, and capers to a hearty base of artichokes and chickpeas. Delicious. Add a dollop of vegan mayo and more fresh dill. Eat it by itself or put it in a sandwich. (Trust us, it works.)

INGREDIENTS

½ cup (100 g) canned artichokes, rinsed and drained

1 cup (170 g) canned chickpeas, rinsed and drained

2 tablespoons fresh dill + more to add on top

½ teaspoon salt, divided

1 tablespoon capers

1 teaspoon lemon juice

1 tablespoon crushed nori

3 tablespoons all-purpose flour

½ cup panko flakes

1 pinch of turmeric

1 tablespoon canola oil

vegan mayo*

INSTRUCTIONS

1. Add the artichokes, chickpeas, dill, ¼ teaspoon of salt, capers, lemon juice, and crushed nori in a food processor and pulse. Add the all-purpose flour and pulse again.
2. In a bowl, add the panko flakes, ¼ teaspoon of salt, and a pinch of turmeric. Combine.
3. Shape the crab cakes and carefully dip all sides in the panko flakes.
4. Heat a pan with the canola oil and bring it to high heat. Add in the crab cakes and let them cook for 5 minutes on each side or until golden and crispy.
5. Serve with a dollop of vegan mayo and more fresh dill on top.

---

*To make a quick vegan mayo, to a bowl add ⅛ cup (30 ml) unsweetened soy milk, ¼ teaspoon apple cider vinegar, ⅛ teaspoon mustard, ⅛ teaspoon maple syrup, ¼ teaspoon salt, and ½ teaspoon lime juice. With an immersion blender mix for 1 minute then slowly drizzle ⅓ cup (80 g) canola oil while the immersion blender is running. Blend 3 minutes until the mayo is thick and creamy. Add more salt, mustard, or lime juice to taste. Store in the fridge for up to 3 days. Add a splash of water to make the mayo easier to drizzle.

SPAGHETTI WITH MEATBALLS

Makes: *35 meatballs* | Time: *55 min*

Another absolute classic comfort food dish—veganized. The meatballs consist of kidney beans, caramelized onion, garlic, oats, spices, and breadcrumbs. They are simply shallow-fried in a pan, no need to turn on the oven for these beauties. Eat them on a salad, in a sandwich, or, as we did, on a bowl of spaghetti with tomato sauce. Yum!

INGREDIENTS FOR MEATBALLS

3 garlic cloves, roughly chopped

1 large red onion, roughly chopped

1½ cups (250 g) canned kidney beans, rinsed and drained

⅓ cup (35 g) rolled oats

1 teaspoon dried basil

1 teaspoon dried oregano

¾ teaspoon salt

¼ cup (40 g) breadcrumbs + more for coating

2 tablespoons olive oil

INGREDIENTS FOR SAUCE

2 garlic cloves, minced

1 red onion, chopped

2 cups (500 g) tomato passata

salt to taste

½ teaspoon dried oregano

½ teaspoon dried basil

ADDITIONAL INGREDIENTS

2 portions cooked spaghetti

cashew Parmesan*

INSTRUCTIONS FOR MEATBALLS

1. Caramelize the chopped garlic cloves and red onion in a lightly oiled pan. Add a pinch of salt to help the softening process. If they start sticking to the pan, add a splash of water and let them cook on medium to high heat for about 5 minutes until softened and brown.
2. To a food processor add the kidney beans, rolled oats, caramelized garlic and onion, spices, and breadcrumbs. Pulse until it all comes together. Scrape down the sides if you need to. You don't want the mixture to be super smooth, but it should stick together.
3. Shape the mixture into 35 meatballs and coat them in breadcrumbs. Let them chill in the fridge while you prepare the sauce. Any leftover meatballs can be frozen and reheated in the oven, microwave, or a pan.

INSTRUCTIONS FOR SAUCE

1. Cook the garlic cloves and red onion in a lightly oiled pot until soft. Then, reduce the heat and add in the tomato passata. Season with salt to taste and add the herbs. Let it cook until hot and thickened just a bit.
2. Coat the bottom of a large pan with oil and pan-fry the meatballs on low to medium heat for about 10 minutes, while flipping them around every couple of minutes or so until they are brown and crispy on all sides.
3. Cook the spaghetti according to package instructions and serve with the meatballs and sauce. Sprinkle with cashew Parmesan for maximum perfection.

---

*For a super quick cashew Parmesan, pulse 1 cup (130 g) cashews, 2 tablespoons nutritional yeast, and ½ teaspoon salt in a food processor until fine.

INDIAN-STYLE BUTTER CHICKEN

Makes: *4 servings* | Time: *40 min*

Did you know you can make delicious vegan Indian-style butter chicken using soy curls? If you don't have these, no problem; this easy-peasy curry can be made with other soy protein, tofu, or even chickpeas. The secret's in the sauce, and if you serve it with some fluffy garlic naan and basmati rice, you get a complete Indian-inspired feast. You deserve it.

INGREDIENTS FOR GARLIC NAAN

1 cup (120 g) all-purpose flour

1 teaspoon baking powder

¼ teaspoon salt + more to sprinkle on top

¼ cup (60 ml) water

2 garlic cloves, peeled and thinly sliced

INGREDIENTS FOR BUTTER CHICKEN

2 cups (80 g) soy curls

2 tablespoons vegan butter

¾ teaspoon salt + ½ teaspoon, divided

¾ teaspoon garam masala + ¼ teaspoon, divided

¾ teaspoon ginger powder + ¼ teaspoon, divided

2 shallots, peeled and diced

2 garlic cloves, peeled and minced

2 cups (500 g) tomato passata

½ cup full-fat coconut milk

fresh cilantro to taste

INSTRUCTIONS FOR GARLIC NAAN

1. Add the flour, baking powder, and salt into a bowl. Stir to combine. Add in the water and knead with your hands or use a stand mixer until a smooth dough forms. If the dough is too sticky, add more flour; if it's too crumbly, add more water. Cover the bowl with a lid or kitchen towel and let the dough rest for a couple of minutes.
2. Divide the naan dough into two pieces and roll each piece out onto a floured surface. Press the garlic slices into each piece of naan.
3. Heat a flat pan (a crepe-pan works best) until really, really hot. Oil the pan and add in one piece of naan at a time garlic-side up for 1 to 2 minutes until brown and bubbly. Flip and cook on the other side for 1 to 2 minutes. Repeat for the other piece of naan. Sprinkle with salt and enjoy!

INSTRUCTIONS FOR BUTTER CHICKEN

1. Fill a pot with water and bring it to a boil. Add in the soy curls and let them cook until soft. Then, drain them, carefully press any excess water out, and set them aside. If you let the curls cool down before cooking the rest of the dish, they will become even more firm and meat-like for maximum awesomeness (if you like that).
2. In a large nonstick pot, add in the vegan butter and bring it to high heat, then add in the soy curls and ¾ teaspoon salt, ¾ teaspoon garam masala, and

(Continued on next page)

¾ teaspoon ginger powder. Stir to combine until the soy curls get brown and crispy.

3. Add shallots to the soy curls and stir. Once the shallots are soft, add in the minced garlic. Cook for another 2 to 3 minutes, then turn down the heat to low.
4. Add in the tomato passata and coconut milk. Stir and add the remaining spices to taste. Let the curry cook until everything is hot and bubbly.
5. Serve with basmati rice and garlic naan, and sprinkle everything with fresh cilantro. You can freeze leftover butter chicken. When ready to eat, simply put the chicken back into a microwave or pot to reheat and it will be good as new.

VEGAN FISH WITH LIME-DILL PEA RICE AND TARTAR SAUCE

Makes: *2 servings (4 fish filets)* | Time: *45 min*

You can make seafood from tofu. Who knew? With this recipe, you will create your very own battered fish filets—without the fish! Finally kick your seafood craving with this plant-based fish dish. Serve with lime-dill pea rice and the special star of the show, our homemade tartar sauce.

INGREDIENTS FOR TARTAR SAUCE

⅛ cup (30 ml) unsweetened soy milk

¼ teaspoon apple cider vinegar

⅛ teaspoon mustard

¼ teaspoon maple syrup

¼ teaspoon kala namak (Himalayan black salt)

½ teaspoon lime juice

⅓ cup (75 g) canola oil

1 teaspoon dill, chopped

1 tablespoon relish

1 teaspoon capers, drained and finely chopped

salt to taste

INGREDIENTS FOR RICE

1 cup (180 g) parboiled rice

1½ cups (375 ml) water

¼ teaspoon salt + more salt to taste

1 cup (115 g) frozen peas

1 tablespoon lime juice

2 teaspoons dill, chopped

INSTRUCTIONS FOR TARTAR SAUCE

1. Add in an immersion blender unsweetened soy milk, apple cider vinegar, mustard, maple syrup, kala namak, and lime juice. Blend for 1 minute, then slowly start drizzling in the canola oil while the immersion blender is running. Blend for about 3 minutes until mixture is thick and creamy. If it's too liquidy, add a bit more oil and blend further.
2. Transfer the mixture to a bowl and add the dill, relish, capers, and more salt to taste. Stir to combine. Set aside in the fridge.

INSTRUCTIONS FOR RICE

1. In a medium-sized pot over low heat, cook the parboiled rice, water, and salt while steaming the frozen peas on top until all the water has been absorbed.
2. Once the rice is done, stir in the peas and add in the lime juice, dill, and more salt to taste. Combine.

INSTRUCTIONS FOR FISH

1. Cut the two slices of tofu in half to make 4 pieces total. Slice the nori sheet into 4 pieces in the same shapes as the tofu pieces. Place the sliced nori pieces on top of each piece of tofu. Press the nori onto each piece of tofu so that it sticks. Sprinkle the backside of each piece of tofu with a pinch of salt.

(Continued on next page)

INGREDIENTS FOR FISH

2 (½ inch or 1 cm–thick) slices firm tofu

1 nori sheet

½ cup (60 g) all-purpose flour

1 tablespoon cornstarch

½ teaspoon salt, divided

¼ teaspoon curry powder

⅛ teaspoon white pepper

½ cup (120 ml) seltzer water or beer or cider

canola oil for pan-frying

2. In a mixing bowl, whisk together the flour, cornstarch, salt, curry powder, and pepper. Then, add in the seltzer water, beer, or cider and whisk until a smooth batter forms. You can adjust the consistency by adding a bit more flour if it's too runny or more seltzer water, beer, or cider if it's too thick.
3. Prepare a pan and fill with enough canola oil so that the fish filets can swim in the oil. Make sure to leave enough space in the pan to prevent the oil from boiling over.
4. Dip the tofu with the nori sheet into the batter, flip until coated on all sides, and put it in the hot pan. Pan-fry for about 3 to 4 minutes on each side until golden.
5. Transfer the vegan fish onto a paper towel to remove excess oil.
6. Serve with the lime-dill pea rice and tartar sauce and enjoy!

PULLED JACKFRUIT TACOS

Makes: *8 tacos* | Time: *30 min*

If you're missing pulled pork tacos in your life, you'll love these pulled jackfruit tacos that we've smothered in deliciously decadent BBQ sauce. It's not always easy to track down canned unripe jackfruit in brine or water, but Asian markets usually have these in stock.

INGREDIENTS FOR PULLED JACKFRUIT

1 teaspoon olive oil

20 oz. (480g) canned unripe jackfruit in brine or water (drained weight: 10 oz. /280 g)

½ teaspoon salt

⅛ teaspoon garlic powder

¼ teaspoon paprika powder

¼ cup (60 ml) water

1 tablespoon tomato paste

⅓ cup (70 g) BBQ sauce

ADDITIONAL INGREDIENTS

8 hard shell tacos*

2 cups (85 g) leafy salad

½ cup (30 g) shredded purple cabbage

2 tablespoons cilantro, chopped

INSTRUCTIONS

1. Add the olive oil to a pan. Drain and rinse the jackfruit, remove the core of the jackfruit (the harder triangular piece) for a better texture, and add the jackfruit to the pan. Pan-fry it for about 4 minutes, then add the salt, garlic power, paprika powder, water, and tomato paste and mix. Let the pulled jackfruit simmer with the lid off for 15 minutes until the water has been absorbed.
2. Use two forks to shred the jackfruit and to create the typical "pulled" look.
3. Pour in the BBQ sauce, give it a good mix, and add additional spices to taste. Let it cook for another minute.

TO ASSEMBLE

1. Add a leafy salad, shredded purple cabbage, and pulled jackfruit onto each hard-shell taco and sprinkle with chopped cilantro.

*A simple trick to make your own hard shell tacos if you only have soft tortillas at home is to fold the soft tortillas over your oven rack and let them bake for 5 to 8 minutes at 350°F/180°C. They should be nice and crispy!

TEX-MEX BURGER

Makes: *6 burgers* | Time: *55 min*

This burger contains many of the typical Tex-Mex staples that will make you full like nothing else: kidney beans, corn, avocado, and tortilla chips. Oh, and lots of cayenne pepper. If you prefer a mild version, you can leave out the cayenne, but if you love the heat, there's really no limit; if it burns your tongue, it's perfect.

INGREDIENTS FOR BURGER PATTIES

1 cup (180 g) canned kidney beans, rinsed and drained

1 cup (180 g) canned corn

1 shallot, peeled

1 garlic clove, peeled

¼ teaspoon cayenne pepper

½ teaspoon salt

¼ cup (40 g) breadcrumbs

¼ cup (25 g) oat flour

¼ cup (35 g) sunflower seeds

all-purpose flour for coating

oil for coating

ADDITIONAL INGREDIENTS

pretzel buns

avocado

ketchup

corn tortilla chips

INSTRUCTIONS

1. Preheat the oven to 400°F/200°C.
2. Add the kidney beans, corn, shallot, and garlic in a food processor and pulse until broken up. Add the spices, breadcrumbs, oat flour, and sunflower seeds and pulse again to combine everything. The mixture should stick together but not be too mushy.
3. Coat your hands in all-purpose flour to shape the burger patties. Lay them on a baking tray lined with parchment paper and spray or coat the patties with oil.
4. Bake in the oven for 30 minutes until golden and crispy, flipping them once after 20 minutes.

TO ASSEMBLE

1. Serve the burger patties in pretzel buns with avocado, ketchup, and crushed corn tortilla chips.

MEATY LASAGNA

Makes: *4 servings* | Time: *80 min*

If you crave lasagna, look no further. This meaty lasagna tastes just like the real deal. The soy granule adds the perfect meaty consistency. With our vegan cheese sauce made from nutritional yeast, this simple yet amazing lasagna is the absolute main event for any lunch or dinner. Pro tip: Make more than you think you'll need.

INGREDIENTS FOR LASAGNA

2 cups (120 g) soy granule (TVP)
½ cup (125 ml) boiling water
1 teaspoon liquid smoke
1¼ teaspoon salt, divided
½ teaspoon paprika powder
¼ teaspoon garlic powder
3 carrots, peeled
1 onion
3 garlic cloves
1 tablespoon olive oil
3 cups tomato passata
1 tablespoon dried oregano
12 sheets oven-ready lasagna sheets

INGREDIENTS FOR CHEESE COATING

2 tablespoons coconut oil or vegan butter
½ teaspoon salt
ground pepper to taste
¼ teaspoon paprika powder
¼ teaspoon curry powder
1 pinch of garlic powder
⅓ cup (40 g) all-purpose flour
⅓ cup (15 g) nutritional yeast
½ cup (120 g) water

INSTRUCTIONS FOR LASAGNA

1. Pour the soy granule in a large bowl and add the boiling water, liquid smoke, ¼ teaspoon salt, paprika powder, and garlic powder. Let the soy granule soak for a few minutes until soft.
2. Preheat the oven to 400°F/200°C.
3. Put the peeled carrots, onion, and garlic cloves in a food processor and chop until small.
4. In a large pot on medium-high heat add in a tablespoon of olive oil followed by the carrot-onion-garlic-mixture. When the onions are cooked through, add in the soft soy granule, tomato passata, 1 teaspoon of salt (use less if using pre-seasoned tomato passata) and the dried oregano. Add more spices to taste. Let the sauce cook for 5 minutes until hot.

INSTRUCTIONS FOR CHEESE COATING

1. While the sauce is cooking, prepare the cheese coating by heating the coconut oil or butter in a small pot over low heat. Add in the salt, pepper, paprika powder, curry powder, and garlic powder. Add in the flour and whisk. Add in nutritional yeast and whisk again until clumpy. Add the water and whisk on low heat for a few minutes until it reaches a gooey consistency. If the sauce is too thick, add more water and whisk again. Set aside.

(Continued on next page)

TO ASSEMBLE

1. When the tomato sauce is ready, start layering the lasagna in a 10 x 18 inch (25 cm x 17 cm) oven dish with one layer of sauce in the baking dish, followed by a layer of cooked lasagna noodles. Repeat until the baking dish is full. The cheese coating should be added as the final layer. Add the nutritional yeast cheese on top and spread it around until the whole top is covered with the cheesy coating.
2. Bake the lasagna in the oven for 30 to 45 minutes until the cheese sauce is golden brown.

SEITAN STEAK

Makes: *2 steaks* | Time: *60 min*

Not unlike meat, seitan can develop every texture from soft and juicy to firm and chewy. This makes seitan an amazing alternative to any meat, which is why in this recipe, we tried our hands at the main event of the meats. By adding sparkling water to the mix, our seitan is softer than many tough store-bought seitan cutlets. It goes perfectly with potatoes, but you can also cut this steak in strips, roast it with some soy sauce, and add it to a sandwich.

INGREDIENTS FOR ROASTED POTATOES

5 medium-sized potatoes

2 teaspoons olive oil

¼ teaspoon salt + more to taste

1 teaspoon dried rosemary

INGREDIENTS FOR HERB BUTTER SPREAD

1 tablespoon vegan butter

1 tablespoon fresh chives, finely cut

1 tablespoon fresh parsley, finely cut

1 pinch salt

INGREDIENTS FOR SEITAN STEAK

½ tablespoon canola oil

½ large white onion, chopped

1 garlic clove, chopped

½ teaspoon cumin seeds

½ teaspoon fennel seeds

¼ cup (40 g) chickpeas

1 tablespoon tomato paste

INSTRUCTIONS FOR ROASTED POTATOES

1. Preheat the oven to 480°F/250°C.
2. Peel (if desired) and cut the potatoes into large chunks.
3. Toss them in olive oil and sprinkle with salt and dried rosemary.
4. Bake them in the oven for 15 to 20 minutes until golden and crispy.

INSTRUCTIONS FOR HERB BUTTER SPREAD

1. Mash together all ingredients. Set aside in the fridge.

INSTRUCTIONS FOR SEITAN STEAK

1. In a large pan with canola oil, sauté the chopped onion and garlic clove until soft. Add in the cumin and fennel seeds and cook until the spices are toasted.
2. In a food processor, add the chickpeas, onion-garlic-spice mixture, tomato paste, salt, thyme, smoked paprika, soy sauce, and sparkling water. Pulse until saucy, then add the vital wheat gluten and pulse again until mixture comes together in a ball.
3. Add a steaming basket to a large pot and fill with a couple of inches of water. Bring the water to a boil.

(Continued on next page)

⅛ teaspoon salt

½ teaspoon thyme

½ teaspoon smoked paprika

1 tablespoon soy sauce

¼ cup (60 ml) sparkling water

¾ cup (90 g) vital wheat gluten

4. Divide the seitan into 2 equal pieces and roll them out with a rolling pin until ½ inch (1–2 cm) thick. Add the seitan filets into the steaming basket and let them steam for about 20 minutes, flipping them after 10 minutes.
5. For perfect grill marks, after steaming cook the seitan steaks for 1 to 2 minutes on each side in a grilling pan. They are delicious topped with the herb butter and served with a side of baked potatoes and BBQ sauce.

SNACKS ARE LOVE; SNACKS ARE LIFE

Sure, you can fill up on a fantastic lunch or dinner, but there's nothing like enjoying a corn dog at a ball game or a load of nachos at a party. We associate certain snacks with good times and great experiences, so we've made it our priority to make these vegan versions just right. Whether you're looking to cut down on your meal sizes, or if you want to make a ton of excellent snacks to impress your friends, we're here to help. Take a bite of our mozzarella sticks, dip a few onion rings into sriracha mayo, or get cozy with some cheesy oven dip. With our veganized snack recipes, you're in for a treat.

EPIC LOADED NACHOS

Makes: *2 servings* | Time: *40 min*

Do you want your friends to like you? With these epic loaded nachos, they will, we promise. (Well, only if you share, that is.) This recipe features an amazing homemade vegan cheese sauce and vegan bacon bits. This is the perfect snack to share. Or frantically devour all by yourself. Who needs friends anyway?

INGREDIENTS FOR VEGAN BACON BITS

½ cup (35 g) soy granule

½ teaspoon liquid smoke

2 teaspoons soy sauce

¼ teaspoon salt

½ teaspoon paprika powder

¼ cup (60 ml) boiling hot water

1 tablespoon canola oil

INGREDIENTS FOR NACHO CHEESE SAUCE

2 tablespoons coconut oil or vegan butter

½ teaspoon salt

ground pepper

¼ teaspoon paprika powder

¼ teaspoon curry powder

1 pinch of garlic powder

⅓ cup (40 g) all-purpose flour

⅓ cup (15 g) nutritional yeast

½ cup (120 g) water

ADDITIONAL INGREDIENTS

1 package (200g) tortilla chips

¼ cup (40 g) canned corn, rinsed and drained

1 avocado, peeled, pitted, and chopped

6 cherry tomatoes, quartered

2 tablespoons scallions, finely chopped

INSTRUCTIONS FOR VEGAN BACON BITS

1. In a bowl, add the soy granule, liquid smoke, soy sauce, salt, and paprika powder. Pour in the hot water and stir to combine. Let the soy granule soak for 5 minutes until soft.
2. In a pan, heat the canola oil and add in the softened soy granule. Cook on medium to high heat until crispy. If the soy granule starts to stick to the pan, add more canola oil.
3. Transfer the granule onto paper towels to remove excess oil.

INSTRUCTIONS FOR NACHO CHEESE SAUCE

1. Heat the coconut oil or butter in a small pot over low heat.
2. Add in the salt, pepper, paprika powder, curry powder, and garlic powder.
3. Add in the flour and whisk, then add in nutritional yeast and whisk again until clumpy.
4. Add in the water and whisk on low heat for a few minutes until cheese sauce gets gooey. If sauce is too thick, add in more water and whisk again.

TO ASSEMBLE

1. Transfer tortilla chips onto a large plate, top with the nacho cheese sauce, vegan bacon bits, corn, avocado, cherry tomatoes, and sprinkle with the chopped scallions. Enjoy!

FISH BITES

Makes: *30–40 fish bites* | Time: *35 min + soaking overnight*

If we told you that the base for these fish bites is just a few slices of potatoes, you'd tell us to finish our beer and go home. We tried a version of this idea when we traveled to Tel Aviv. Since then, we've been trying to recreate the recipe and make our own version of this amazing street food that tastes so much like the perfect combination of fish and chips. While the dill, lemon juice, and crushed nori give these bites their delicious fishy flavor, adding some sparkling water in the batter will make the dough crisp and light.

INGREDIENTS FOR FISH BITES

2 smallish potatoes

½ cup (60 g) all-purpose flour

1 tablespoon cornstarch

½ teaspoon salt + more to sprinkle on top

2 tablespoons crushed nori sheet

¼ teaspoon dried dill + more to sprinkle on top

⅓ cup (100 ml) + 1 tablespoon sparkling water, divided

oil for frying

lemon juice to squeeze on top

INGREDIENTS FOR CASHEW LEMON DIP

1 cup (130 g) raw, unsalted cashews (soaked overnight; see instructions)

⅓ cup (80 g) water

3 tablespoons lemon juice

½ teaspoon salt

1 teaspoon maple syrup

1 pinch turmeric

INSTRUCTIONS FOR FISH BITES

1. Peel the potatoes and slice them as thin as possible. You should end up with about 30 to 40 slices.
2. Combine the flour, cornstarch, salt, crushed nori, and dried dill. Add in 1 cup sparkling water and whisk until a thick batter forms.
3. Heat the frying oil in a pot or deep fryer to 350°F/175°C. Dip each potato slice into the batter before carefully letting the slices slide into the oil. It's best to work in batches in order not to overcrowd the pot. Fry the fish bites for 3 minutes per side until golden and crispy. Repeat until all potato slices are fried.
4. Transfer the fried potato slices onto paper towels to remove excess oil, then add all the fish bites into a bowl, sprinkle more salt and dill on top, and add a generous squeeze of lemon juice. Shake to combine.
5. Potato chips and a cashew lemon dip are the ideal side dishes for these yummy fishy bites!

INSTRUCTIONS FOR CASHEW LEMON DIP

1. Soak the cashews in water overnight. The next day, rinse and drain the cashews.
2. After soaking overnight, add the cashews to water, lemon juice, salt, maple syrup, and turmeric in a blender and blend until completely smooth. You might have to scrape down the sides a couple of times.

(Continued on next page)

INGREDIENTS FOR CHIPS

2 potatoes

1 teaspoon olive oil

¼ teaspoon salt

⅛ teaspoon pepper

INSTRUCTIONS FOR CHIPS

1. Preheat the oven to 480°F/250°C.
2. Peel the potatoes and cut them in wedges. Coat them with olive oil, salt, and pepper.
3. Transfer them to a baking tray lined with parchment paper and bake them in the oven for 15 to 20 minutes until golden and crispy.

MOZZARELLA STICKS

Makes: *25–30 Mozzarella sticks* | Time: *45 min + soaking overnight + 2 hours chill time*

Oh, how we used to love mozzarella sticks before we went vegan. Naturally, it was one of the worst cravings we had, until we discovered how to make our very own dairy-free vegan mozzarella sticks with homemade cashew mozzarella! Tip for the lazy: If you want to skip making your own cheese, use a block of store-bought vegan cheese that melts when hot.

INGREDIENTS FOR CASHEW MOZZARELLA

1 cup (130 g) raw, unsalted cashews (soaked overnight; see instructions)

4 teaspoons tapioca starch

2 small garlic cloves

4 tablespoons nutritional yeast

¾ teaspoon salt

1 tablespoon lemon juice

½ cup (125 ml) water

INGREDIENTS FOR MOZZARELLA STICKS

½ cup (60 g) chickpea or all-purpose flour

1 teaspoon kala namak (Himalayan black salt)

½ cup + 1 tablespoon (130 ml) water

1 cup (60 g) panko flakes

¼ cup (40 g) breadcrumbs

¾ teaspoon salt

1 teaspoon dried rosemary

½ teaspoon paprika powder

INSTRUCTIONS FOR CASHEW MOZZARELLA

1. Soak the cashews in water overnight. The next day, rinse and drain the cashews.
2. After soaking overnight, place the cashews and all other cashew mozzarella ingredients in a blender and blend until completely smooth. You might have to scrape down the sides a few times.
3. Transfer the cheese mixture into a saucepan and bring to medium heat. Keep stirring for 3 to 4 minutes until a stretchy consistency is formed. Then, transfer the cheese into a container and let it cool off. Let it chill in the fridge for at least 1 hour and then in the freezer for another hour after that.
4. Cut the mozzarella into slices and then into sticks.

INSTRUCTIONS FOR MOZZARELLA STICKS

1. Whisk together the chickpea flour, kala namak, and ½ cup water. You might have to add a bit more water or flour to reach the right egg-like consistency.
2. In a separate bowl whisk together the panko flakes, breadcrumbs, and spices.
3. Heat the frying oil in a pot to 350°F/175°C. Dip each mozzarella stick first into the batter, then into the breading. Make sure they are coated on all sides.

(Continued on next page)

½ teaspoon curry powder
¼ teaspoon onion powder
¼ teaspoon garlic powder

ADDITIONAL INGREDIENTS

oil for frying

Carefully lower each mozzarella stick into the oil and fry until golden and crispy. Work in batches until all mozzarella sticks are fried.

4. Transfer mozzarella sticks to paper towels to remove excess oil. Serve them with a simple tomato dip*.

*To make our tomato dip, simply whisk together ¼ cup (65 g) tomato passata, dried basil, dried oregano, salt, garlic powder, and cracked black pepper to taste.

CORN DOGS

Makes: *12 mini corn dogs* | Time: *70 min*

This delicious and simple-looking snack is such a classic and beloved street food, we had to include it in this book. With this recipe, you will finally be able to create a plant-based version from scratch. Made with our homemade seitan sausages and crispy corn batter, these corn dogs taste just as good as the ones you'd get at a fair.

INGREDIENTS FOR SEITAN SAUSAGES*

½ tablespoon canola oil

½ large white onion, chopped

1 garlic clove, chopped

½ teaspoon cumin seeds

½ teaspoon fennel seeds

¼ cup (40 g) chickpeas

1 tablespoon tomato paste

⅛ teaspoon salt

½ teaspoon thyme

½ teaspoon smoked paprika

1 tablespoon soy sauce

¼ cup (60 ml) sparkling water

¾ cup (90 g) vital wheat gluten

INGREDIENTS FOR CORN BATTER

½ cup (90 g) fine cornmeal

½ cup (80 g) all-purpose flour

1 teaspoon salt

¼ teaspoon black pepper

½ teaspoon baking powder

½ teaspoon white sugar

INSTRUCTIONS FOR SEITAN SAUSAGES

1. In a large pan with canola oil, sauté the chopped onion and garlic until soft. Add the cumin and fennel seeds and cook further until the spices are toasted.
2. In a food processor, add the chickpeas, onion-garlic-spice mixture, tomato paste, salt, thyme, smoked paprika, soy sauce, and sparkling water. Pulse until saucy, then add the vital wheat gluten and pulse again until it comes together in a ball.
3. Add a steaming basket to a large pot and fill with a couple of inches of water. Bring the water to a boil.
4. Divide the seitan into 4 equal chunks. Roll and press the seitan into a sausage shape. Roll each sausage in parchment paper and aluminum foil. Twist the ends so that the seitan is completely closed off. Add the seitan sausages into the steaming basket and let them steam for about 40 minutes, flipping them after 20 minutes.
5. Let them cool off a bit before removing the aluminum foil and parchment paper.
6. Cut each sausage into 3 equal parts and stick a popsicle stick (or similar stick like a cake pop stick) into each piece.

INSTRUCTIONS FOR CORN BATTER

1. Combine all the dry ingredients, then add in the plant-based milk and whisk until a smooth batter is formed.

(Continued on next page)

*Not in the mood for making your own seitan? To save time you can also use store-bought vegan sausages.

½ cup (125 ml) unsweetened plant-based milk, e.g., rice milk

oil for frying

Fill the batter into a tall glass.

2. Heat the frying oil in a pot or deep fryer. Dip each sausage piece into the corn batter (you might have to add more flour if it's too runny or more milk if it's too thick) and then carefully fry the corn dogs (work in batches) for 2 to 3 minutes until the corn batter is golden and crispy.
3. Transfer the corn dogs to a kitchen paper to remove excess oil.
4. Serve with ketchup or mustard.

SOFT PRETZEL BITES WITH CIDER CHEESE DIP

Makes: *2–3 servings* | Time: *50 min + 2 hours rising time*

Cider, cheese, and pretzels. So wrong, yet so beautifully right. These soft pretzel bites will keep your friends coming back for more. Add them to our deliciously tangy cider cheese dip, and you will never be lonely and/or hungry again.

INGREDIENTS FOR PRETZEL BITES

1¼ cups (150 g) all-purpose flour + more for dusting

½ teaspoon instant yeast

⅛ teaspoon salt

1 teaspoon olive oil + more to coat the dough

⅓ cup (85 ml) + 3 cups (750 ml) water, divided

1½ tablespoons baking soda

2 teaspoons pretzel salt

INGREDIENTS FOR CIDER CHEESE DIP

1 tablespoon coconut oil, melted (or vegan butter)

¼ teaspoon salt

⅛ teaspoon turmeric powder

⅛ teaspoon curry powder

1 tablespoon all-purpose flour

1 tablespoon nutritional yeast

¼ cup (60 ml) cider

½ teaspoon maple syrup

INSTRUCTIONS FOR PRETZEL BITES

1. Combine the flour, instant yeast, and salt in a mixing bowl. Add olive oil and ⅓ cup water. Mix and knead by hand until a soft dough forms or put all the ingredients in a kitchen machine and let the machine knead the dough for you. This will take 4 to 5 minutes. Fine-tune the mixture: If it's too sticky, add more flour. If it's too crumbly, add more water.
2. Coat the ball of dough with a drizzle of olive oil. Cover the bowl with a clean kitchen towel and let the dough rest in a warm spot for 2 to 3 hours (depending on room temperature) until it doubles in size.
3. Preheat the oven to 400°F/200°C.
4. Divide the dough into 4 equal parts, roll them into ropes, and cut them into bite-sized pieces.
5. In a medium-sized pot, bring the remaining 3 cups water to a boil. Add in the baking soda and stir to combine.
6. Work in batches to cook all the pretzel bites in the baking soda bath for 1 minute. Then, transfer them to a baking tray lined with parchment paper and sprinkle them with pretzel salt.
7. Bake them in the oven for 15 to 20 minutes until golden and serve with a side of cider cheese dip. You've waited long enough. Dig in!

(Continued on next page)

INSTRUCTIONS FOR CIDER CHEESE DIP

1. Heat the coconut oil or butter in a small pot over low heat. Add the salt, turmeric powder, and curry powder. Add in the flour and whisk. Add nutritional yeast and whisk again until clumpy.
2. Add in the cider and maple syrup and whisk on low heat for a few minutes until creamy. If it gets too thick, add more water or cider and whisk again to make it smooth and creamy. Set aside until pretzel bites are ready to serve.

BBQ CAULIFLOWER WINGS

Makes: *2 servings* | Time: *45 min*

Do you ever miss boneless wings? If you are a sports person, or just a lover of game-day eats, these fried BBQ Cauliflower Wings are the perfect game-day snack or party food. Smother them in BBQ sauce and dip them in ranch dip or vegan mayo until you've been eating them all by yourself and the game is over and you wonder where all that time with friends went.

INGREDIENTS FOR CAULIFLOWER WINGS

½ head (400 g) cauliflower
1¼ cups (150 g) flour
1 cup (240 ml) water
½ teaspoon salt
¼ teaspoon paprika powder
⅛ teaspoon garlic powder
ground pepper
oil for frying

INGREDIENTS FOR BBQ SAUCE

3 tablespoons vegan BBQ sauce
2 tablespoons water

INSTRUCTIONS FOR CAULIFLOWER WINGS

1. Break down the cauliflower into florets of approximately the same size.
2. Combine the flour, water, salt, paprika powder, garlic powder, and ground pepper into a thick batter.
3. Heat the frying oil in a pot (if you use a smaller pot you can use less oil but you have to work in more batches, and make sure not to fill the pot with too much oil to prevent it from boiling over) or deep fryer to 350°F/175°C.
4. Once the oil is hot, dip one cauliflower floret after another into the batter. Let them fry for 4 to 5 minutes until florets are golden and crispy. Set them aside on paper towels to let excess oil drip off. Repeat until all the cauliflower wings are fried.

INSTRUCTIONS FOR BBQ SAUCE

1. Thin out the BBQ sauce by adding the water until you can easily drizzle it.
2. Put all the cauliflower wings in a large bowl, add the BBQ sauce, and toss until all wings are coated. They are the best when served fresh! A ranch dip or vegan mayo* are the ideal dipping sauces.

---

*To make a quick vegan mayo, to a bowl add ⅛ cup (30 ml) unsweetened soy milk, ¼ teaspoon apple cider vinegar, ⅛ teaspoon mustard, ⅛ teaspoon maple syrup, ¼ teaspoon salt, and ½ teaspoon lime juice. With an immersion blender mix for 1 minute then slowly drizzle ⅓ cup (80 g) canola oil while the immersion blender is running. Blend 3 minutes until the mayo is thick and creamy. Add more salt, mustard, or lime juice to taste. Store in the fridge for up to 3 days. Add a splash of water to make the mayo easier to drizzle.

CASHEW CHEESE WHEEL

Makes: *1 cheese wheel* | Time: *20 min + soaking overnight*

Once your cashews have been soaked, this no-cook, no-bake raw cashew cheese wheel only takes a few minutes to prepare. You won't believe how spreadable yet firm it is. Keep some crackers or fresh bread on hand 'cause this cheese goes well with many things and will become an obligatory part of your vegan party platter.

INGREDIENTS

1 cup (150 g) raw, unsalted cashews (soaked overnight; see instructions)

1 small garlic clove

1 teaspoon lemon zest

1 tablespoon lemon juice

¼ teaspoon salt

2 tablespoons nutritional yeast

1 teaspoon olive oil

3 tablespoons pistachios, chopped

INSTRUCTIONS

1. Soak the cashews in water overnight. Rinse and drain.
2. To a food processor add the soaked cashews and all other ingredients except the chopped pistachios. Pulse until fine and creamy. You might have to scrape down the sides a couple of times.
3. Now, transfer the cashew cheese onto parchment paper and use the sides of the parchment paper to help shape a wheel.
4. Let the cheese wheel chill in the fridge for 2 to 3 hours until it firms up.
5. Pour the chopped pistachios onto a plate and carefully coat the cashew cheese on all sides with the pistachios.
6. Enjoy this vegan cashew cheese wheel with crackers, veggies, or bread. Leftovers can be stored in the fridge for 2 to 3 days.

BEER-BATTERED ONION RINGS WITH SRIRACHA MAYO

Makes: *2 servings* | Time: *40 min*

So many beautiful words in this recipe's name. With this recipe, we tell you how to make your own vegan onion rings with a light, tempura-like batter, but we also tell you how to make vegan sriracha mayo, which you can (and should) use for everything.

INGREDIENTS FOR ONION RINGS

1 large white onion

1 cup (125 g) all-purpose flour

2 tablespoons cornstarch

1 teaspoon salt

¼ teaspoon paprika powder

⅛ teaspoon white pepper

1 cup (250 ml) beer*

oil for frying

INGREDIENTS FOR SRIRACHA MAYO

⅛ cup (30 ml) unsweetened soy milk

¼ teaspoon apple cider vinegar

⅛ teaspoon mustard

¼ teaspoon maple syrup

¼ teaspoon kala namak (Himalayan black salt)

½ teaspoon lime juice

⅓ cup (80 g) canola oil

¼ teaspoon sriracha

INSTRUCTIONS FOR ONION RINGS

1. Peel the onion, cut it into ½-inch (1–2 cm) slices, and separate the rings.
2. In a mixing bowl, whisk together the flour, cornstarch, salt, paprika powder, and white pepper. Add in the beer (or sparkling water) and whisk until a smooth batter is formed. You can adjust the consistency by adding more flour if it's too runny or more beer or sparkling water if it's too thick.
3. Heat the frying oil in a large pot to 350°F/175 °C. You won't need much oil, but the onion rings should swim in it.
4. Dip the onion rings into the batter and immediately add them to the oil. Work in batches to prevent overcrowding in the pot.
5. Let the onion rings cook for 3 to 4 minutes until golden and crispy.
6. Transfer the onion rings onto paper towels to remove excess oil. Sprinkle them with more salt and enjoy with the sriracha mayo.

INSTRUCTIONS FOR SRIRACHA MAYO

1. Blend the following ingredients using an immersion blender: unsweetened soy milk, apple cider vinegar, mustard, maple syrup, kala namak, and lime juice. Blend for 1 minute then slowly start drizzling in the canola oil while the immersion blender is running. Blend for about 3 minutes until the mayo is thick and creamy. If it's too liquidy, add a bit more oil and blend further.
2. Add in the sriracha and blend again. You can add more salt, mustard, sriracha, or lime juice to taste. Store mayo in the fridge for up to 3 days.

---

*If you don't want to use beer in this batter, you can use sparkling water instead.

CHILI CHEESE FRIES

Makes: *2 servings* | Time: *110 min*

Do you eat your chili cheese fries with your fingers or a fork? However you choose to gobble down, we've made sure that you will enjoy our vegan twist on this classic beauty. The mean chili, the creamy cheese sauce, the golden fries: everything is made from scratch in this recipe.

INGREDIENTS FOR FRIES

3 large potatoes

1 tablespoon olive oil

¼ teaspoon salt + more to taste

ground black pepper

INGREDIENTS FOR CHILI*

1 teaspoon olive oil

2 red onions, chopped

4 garlic cloves, minced

15 oz. (425 g) canned corn, rinsed and drained

15 oz. (425 g) canned kidney beans, rinsed and drained

2 cups (500 ml) water

1 teaspoon paprika powder

1 teaspoon salt + more to taste

1 teaspoon chili powder + more to taste

2 teaspoons cocoa powder

1 cup (250 g) tomato passata

INGREDIENTS FOR CHEESE SAUCE

2 tablespoons coconut oil or vegan butter

INSTRUCTIONS FOR FRIES

1. Preheat the oven to 400°F/200°C.
2. Wash the potatoes and peel them if desired. Cut them by hand or with a french fry cutter into equally sized fries.
3. Add the fries into a large bowl, then add in the olive oil, salt, and black pepper. Toss to coat.
4. Add the fries to a baking tray lined with parchment paper. The fries should not touch each other on the paper.
5. Bake the fries in the oven for 15 to 20 minutes until golden and crispy.

INSTRUCTIONS FOR CHILI

1. In a big pot with the olive oil, add in the chopped onions and minced garlic and let them cook on medium heat for a few minutes until translucent.
2. Add in the corn, kidney beans, water, paprika powder, salt, chili powder, cocoa powder, and tomato passata. Give the pot a quick stir, put the lid on, and let the chili cook for about 30 minutes on medium heat. The chili should thicken quite nicely. If the water has cooked down too much, you can add more water or tomato passata. Let the chili cook without the lid on for another 5 to 10 minutes until it has reached the right consistency.

(Continued on next page)

*You won't need all the chili for these chili cheese fries, but the leftovers freeze well.

½ teaspoon salt

⅛ teaspoon turmeric powder

¼ teaspoon curry powder

¼ teaspoon paprika powder

⅓ cup (40 g) all-purpose flour

⅓ cup (15 g) nutritional yeast

½ cup (120 g) water

ADDITIONAL INGREDIENT

1 tablespoon scallions, thinly sliced

INSTRUCTIONS FOR CHEESE SAUCE

1. Heat the coconut oil or butter in a small pot over low heat.
2. Add the salt, turmeric powder, curry powder, and paprika powder.
3. Add in the flour and whisk. Then, add in the nutritional yeast and whisk again until clumpy.
4. Add in the water and whisk on low heat for 1 to 2 minutes until the cheese sauce gets gooey. If the sauce is too thick, add more water and whisk again. Set aside until fries are ready to serve.

TO ASSEMBLE

1. Top the fries with the chili, cheese sauce, and thinly sliced scallions, take a photo to impress your friends, and dig in!

VEGAN CHICKEN-STYLE NUGGETS

Makes: *16 nuggets* | Time: *60 min*

Yes, it can be done. This is a recipe for amazing chicken-style nuggets made with seitan, but this isn't your typical seitan; it's super fluffy because it's made with sparkling water. Oh, you're gonna love this. Nugget. Dip. Bite. Repeat.

INGREDIENTS FOR ORANGE DIPPING SAUCE

⅓ cup (80 ml) orange juice

½ tablespoon brown sugar

½ teaspoon tomato paste

½ teaspoon apple cider vinegar

⅛ teaspoon salt + more to taste

½ tablespoon cornstarch

½ tablespoon water

INGREDIENTS FOR NUGGETS

½ tablespoon canola oil + extra for pan frying

½ large white onion, chopped

1 garlic clove, chopped

½ teaspoon cumin seeds

½ teaspoon fennel seeds

¼ cup (40 g) chickpeas

1 tablespoon tomato paste

⅛ teaspoon salt

½ teaspoon thyme

½ teaspoon smoked paprika

1 tablespoon soy sauce

¼ cup (60 ml) sparkling water

INSTRUCTIONS FOR ORANGE DIPPING SAUCE

1. In a saucepan, combine the orange juice, brown sugar, tomato paste, apple cider vinegar, and salt. Give it a mix and let it cook on medium heat until the sugar has dissolved.
2. In a separate bowl, whisk together the cornstarch and water and pour it into the sauce. Whisk until combined and the orange dipping sauce has thickened. Set aside.

INSTRUCTIONS FOR NUGGETS

1. In a large pan with canola oil, sauté the chopped onion and garlic until soft. Add the cumin and fennel seeds and cook further until the spices are toasted.
2. In a food processor, add the chickpeas, onion-garlic-spice mixture, tomato paste, salt, thyme, smoked paprika, soy sauce, and sparkling water. Pulse until saucy, then add the vital wheat gluten and pulse again until it comes together in a ball.
3. Add a steaming basket to a large pot and fill with a couple of inches of water. Bring the water to a boil.
4. Divide the seitan into 16 equal pieces and press those pieces flat into nugget shapes. Add the seitan nuggets into the steaming basket and let them steam for about 20 minutes, flipping them after 10.
5. Combine the chickpea flour, water, and sriracha sauce in one bowl and whisk until smooth.

(Continued on next page)

¾ cup (90 g) vital wheat gluten

¾ cup (90 g) chickpea flour

½ cup (125 ml) water

¼ teaspoon sriracha

½ cup (65 g) breadcrumbs

½ cup (30 g) panko flakes

3 tablespoons white sesame seeds

1 teaspoon chicken seasoning*

6. Combine the breadcrumbs, panko flakes, white sesame seeds, and chicken seasoning in another bowl.
7. Once the steamed nuggets are soft, let them cool off a bit. Now, first dip them in the egg replacement, then in the breading. Repeat until all seitan nuggets are coated.
8. Cover the bottom of a pan with canola oil for frying. Pan-fry the nuggets for 3 to 4 minutes per side until golden and crisp and awesome-looking. Serve with the orange dipping sauce.

*Make your own chicken seasoning by combining 1 teaspoon salt, ½ teaspoon paprika, ⅛ teaspoon pepper, and ⅛ teaspoon garlic powder.

CHEESY OVEN DIP WITH GARLIC HERB BAGUETTE

Makes: *4 servings** | Time: *50 min + soaking overnight*

Even as vegans we have to admit, there's lots of comfort in cheese dip. There's nothing like a warm cheese dip fresh out of the oven—except a warm cheese dip served on a garlic herb baguette. When this recipe worked as it did, we knew we'd have to share it with the world. Or at least with whoever reads this, which is you. Hi!

INGREDIENTS FOR CHEESY OVEN DIP

1 cup (130 g) raw, unsalted cashews (soaked overnight; see instructions)
4 teaspoons tapioca starch
2 small garlic cloves
4 tablespoons nutritional yeast
¾ teaspoon salt
2 teaspoons lemon juice
½ cup (125 ml) water
1 pinch cayenne pepper

INGREDIENTS FOR GARLIC HERB BAGUETTE

1 baguette
3 tablespoons olive oil
1 garlic clove, minced
½ teaspoon dried oregano
½ teaspoon dried basil
¼ teaspoon salt

INSTRUCTIONS FOR CHEESY OVEN DIP

1. Soak the cashews in water overnight. The next day, rinse and drain the cashews.
2. After cashews are soaked, preheat the oven to 400°F/200°C.
3. Place all the ingredients for the cheesy oven dip (except the cayenne pepper) in a blender and blend until completely smooth. You might have to scrape down the sides a few times.
4. Transfer the cheese mixture into 2 (3½ inch or 9 cm) baking dishes lined with parchment paper.
5. Bake the cheesy dip for 25 to 30 minutes until it is slightly golden on top.
6. Sprinkle cayenne pepper on top of the cheesy oven dip and enjoy with the warm baguette!

INSTRUCTIONS FOR GARLIC HERB BAGUETTE

1. Cut the baguette in half and slice each half open lengthwise.
2. Mix the olive oil with the minced garlic, oregano, basil, and salt. Brush the inside of the baguette with the oil mixture.
3. Bake the baguette together with the cheese dip on top for the last 10 minutes to make it warm and delicious.

---

*With the ingredients given you'll be able to fill 2 (3½ inch or 9 cm) baking dishes. If you're using a blender with a small container, feel free to halve the cheesy oven dip ingredients to make only one dish.

VEGANISM IS TOTALLY SWEET

While we are really big on savory vegan food, sometimes we get cravings for a sugary treat. Chocolate, ice cream, cookies, cake, you name it, we crave it. But that's not always easy. Most classic desserts and sweets aren't exactly vegan by default, so chances are your favorite apple pie has eggs, that awesome banana chocolate chip ice cream you love is made with cream, and the panna cotta you always ordered at the Italian place is made with all the dairy in the world. In the mood for churros or classic chocolate donuts? Been trying to make your mamma's favorite apple fritters? We've got some good news for you. Almost every dessert recipe can easily be veganized.

CLASSIC APPLE PIE

Makes: *1 pie in a 7½-inch (19 cm) tart pan* | Time: *75 min*

Making apple pie from scratch may sound intimidating, but we guarantee this one will turn out instantly amazing on the first try. Neither the filling nor the crust is hard to make, and science says that being able to make a classic apple pie makes you a cool cat.

INGREDIENTS FOR FILLING

4 (500 g) sweet apples

1 tablespoon coconut oil

2 tablespoons brown sugar

¾ teaspoon cinnamon powder

¼ teaspoon ginger powder

1 tablespoon almond butter

INGREDIENTS FOR CRUST

1 cup (125 g) whole wheat flour

1 cup (125 g) all-purpose flour

2 tablespoons brown sugar

1 pinch of salt

⅓ cup (65 g) coconut oil + more for brushing the top

6 tablespoons ice water

INSTRUCTIONS FOR FILLING

1. Preheat the oven to 400°F/200°C.
2. Peel the apples, cut into quarters, remove the core, and cut each quarter into four slices. Heat the coconut oil in a large pan and add in the apples, sugar, cinnamon, and ginger powder. Stir until the apples are coated evenly. Let them cook for about 2 minutes on medium to high heat, then reduce the heat to a simmer and let the apples cook further, for about 10 minutes, with the pan lid on.

INSTRUCTIONS FOR CRUST

1. Add the whole wheat flour, all-purpose flour, brown sugar, and salt in a food processor. Pulse to combine. Add the coconut oil tablespoon by tablespoon and pulse in between. Once the coconut oil is used up, add the ice water by the tablespoon and pulse in between. The dough should stick together if you pinch it between two fingers. You might have to add a bit more water to achieve that.
2. Divide the crust into two parts and roll it out onto parchment paper. Transfer the first layer of the crust onto a 7½-inch (19 cm) tart pan.
3. Mix the almond butter into the apples and transfer the filling into the baking pan with the crust.
4. Roll out the second crust and add it on top. Pinch together the edges. With a knife, make 4 incisions on the top crust to let the filling breathe while baking.
5. Bake the pie for 30 to 35 minutes in the oven. Brush the crust twice with coconut oil, approximately 1 minute before taking it out of the oven, and again after baking for a nice glossy finish.
6. Allow the cake to cool off before digging in. Sure, warm pie is great, but this classic apple pie is even better the day after. Store it in the fridge for up to 2 days.

SOFT-BAKED CHOCOLATE COOKIES

Makes: *8 cookies* | Time: *25 min*

What if we told you there is a way to make soft-baked, fudgy, crisp on the outside chocolate cookies with all plant-based ingredients? These soft-baked chocolate cookies are a staple for desserts, afternoon tea times, or coffee breaks. To make them, you'll only need a handful of basic ingredients and less than an hour.

INGREDIENTS

⅓ cup (70g) coconut oil, softened at room temperature

⅓ cup (65g) white sugar (make sure it's vegan!)

1¼ cups (170g) all-purpose flour

½ teaspoon baking powder

2 tablespoons cocoa powder

6 tablespoons almond milk or other plant-based milk

1 tablespoon vegan chocolate chips

INSTRUCTIONS

1. Preheat the oven to 360°F/180°C.
2. In a mixing bowl, add the softened coconut oil and white sugar. Mix everything with a hand mixer or a stand mixer.
3. Add in the flour, baking powder, and cocoa powder and mix again. Then, add in the almond milk until everything comes together.
4. Divide the dough into 8 equal pieces, form balls with your hands, and press them flat to about ½ inch (1 cm) onto a baking tray lined with parchment paper. Press a few chocolate chips into each cookie.
5. Bake the cookies in the oven for 8 to 10 minutes. They will feel pretty soft at first, but after cooling for a couple of minutes, they should have the perfect texture.

QUICK BANANA BREAD MUFFINS

Makes: *8 muffins* | Time: *35 min*

We all love banana bread, but why does it have to take so long to make? These banana bread muffins are the obvious solution to a problem that needed solving for a long time. What a great treat to start the day.

INGREDIENTS

2 ripe bananas, peeled

1 tablespoon maple syrup

½ cup (125 ml) plant-based milk, e.g., rice coconut milk

¼ teaspoon apple cider vinegar

1 tablespoon coconut oil, melted

1 cup (125 ml) all-purpose flour

¼ cup (25 g) hazelnut meal (save a bit to sprinkle on top right before baking)

1 teaspoon baking powder

¼ teaspoon baking soda

⅓ cup (50 g) chocolate chunks (save a few to add on top right before baking)

INSTRUCTIONS

1. Preheat the oven to 350°F/180°C.
2. In a large bowl, mash the bananas. Add the maple syrup, plant-based milk, apple cider vinegar, and coconut oil. Whisk to combine.
3. To the same bowl, add the flour, hazelnut meal, baking powder, and baking soda. Stir to combine. It should be a thick batter.
4. Add in about ¾ of the chocolate chunks. Stir to combine.
5. Scoop the batter into a muffin pan lined with muffin papers or silicone forms. The batter should be enough for 8 muffins. Divide the rest of the chocolate chunks among the muffins.
6. Bake for 20 to 25 minutes until golden on top. You can use a toothpick or small wooden stick to check if the muffins are baked all the way through. Let them cool off a bit before digging in, then dig in deep and never stop.

CHUBBY CHIMP ICE CREAM

Makes: *2 servings* | Time: *15 min*

If you like peanut butter, chocolate, walnuts, or all of the above, then you're in for a treat with this awesome combination. Just a scoop (or five) of our chubby chimp ice cream will give you an extra tasty boost on hot summer days. Pro tip: Always keep banana chunks in your freezer so you can make this recipe anytime in just a few minutes.

INGREDIENTS

3 frozen bananas, peeled and cut in chunks

¼ cup (40 g) peanut butter

¼ cup (40 g) chopped chocolate

¼ cup (25 g) chopped walnuts

INSTRUCTIONS

1. Add the frozen bananas in a food processor and pulse until creamy (this can take a while, don't give up; scrape down the sides if necessary).
2. Add in the peanut butter and pulse until it's incorporated into the ice cream. I still like peanut butter bits in the ice cream, so I don't pulse too much.
3. Add in the chopped chocolate and walnuts and pulse to combine everything.
4. Scoop the chubby chip ice cream into bowls and enjoy!

CHOCOLATE-COCONUT DONUTS

Makes: *8 donuts* | Time: *90 min + 1–2 hours rising time*

Fluffy and soft on the inside, crisp and golden on the outside. That's what we've come to expect from our donuts, and that's what we worked toward when creating this recipe. No twists, no surprises. Our vegan donuts are coated with a classic chocolate glaze and sprinkled with coconut flakes.

INGREDIENTS FOR DONUTS

½ cup (125 g) plant-based milk (e.g., coconut rice milk)

1 tablespoon coconut oil

2 cups (250 g) all-purpose flour

2 tablespoons white sugar (make sure it's vegan!)

1 teaspoon instant yeast

oil for frying

INGREDIENTS FOR GLAZE AND TOPPINGS

⅓ cup (60 g) chocolate chips or baking chocolate

1 teaspoon coconut oil

1 tablespoon coconut flakes

INSTRUCTIONS FOR DONUTS

1. Heat the plant-based milk and coconut oil in a small pot until the coconut oil is melted, then let it cool down to room temperature (it shouldn't feel too warm). If the mixture is too hot, you'll kill the yeast and the dough will not rise.
2. Combine the flour, sugar, and instant yeast in a large mixing bowl, then add the cooled oil and milk mixture. Combine and knead (or let a stand mixer with a dough hook knead it) until a smooth dough forms. If the dough is too sticky, add more flour. Cover the bowl with a clean kitchen towel and let it rise for 1 to 2 hours until the dough doubles in size.
3. Roll out the dough onto a lightly floured surface to about ½-inch thickness. Use a glass to cut out the donuts and a glass bottle opening to cut out the donut hole.
4. Heat your frying oil to 350°F/175°C: You can use a deep-fryer if you have one or a pot filled with just enough oil so that the donuts can swim in it. Make sure not to add too much oil in the pot because the oil will rise and you don't want an accident to happen. Fry the donuts on each side until golden brown.
5. Transfer the donuts to a paper towel to remove excess oil. Let them cool off before applying the chocolate glaze.

INSTRUCTIONS FOR GLAZE AND TOPPINGS

1. In a double boiler, melt the chocolate and coconut oil. Stir to combine.
2. Dip each donut into the chocolate glaze, sprinkle with coconut flakes, and let them cool off until the chocolate has set.

PINEAPPLE-COCONUT STREUSEL CAKE

Makes: *6 servings* | Time: *50 min*

In the mood for a tropical treat? In this recipe, we've combined a summery mix of fresh pineapples and desiccated coconut with a classic streusel cake topping. It's quite easy to make and highly customizable. Try versions with peaches, plums, rhubarb, or pretty much any fruit. Anything goes, and almost everything will work.

INGREDIENTS FOR CAKE

1⅓ cup (160 g) all-purpose flour

½ cup (40 g) desiccated coconut

½ cup (100 g) white sugar

1½ teaspoons baking powder

½ teaspoon baking soda

1 tablespoon coconut oil, liquid

½ teaspoon apple cider vinegar

¼ teaspoon vanilla extract

¾ cup (180 ml) lukewarm water

1 cup (220 g) pineapple chunks (fresh or canned)

INGREDIENTS FOR STREUSEL

¼ cup (50 g) cold vegan butter

⅔ cup (80 g) all-purpose flour

¼ cup (50 g) white sugar

INSTRUCTIONS FOR CAKE

1. Preheat the oven to 360°F/180°C.
2. Place all the dry ingredients for the cake base in a mixing bowl and combine. Add the wet ingredients except the pineapple chunks and whisk until a smooth batter is formed.
3. Lightly oil a 10 x 8 inch (26 x 20 cm) baking pan and pour in the cake batter. Spread the pineapple chunks evenly across the top of the mixture and press them a bit into the mixture.

INSTRUCTIONS FOR STREUSEL

1. Add the cold butter, all-purpose flour, and sugar in a bowl and mix and knead with your fingers or a fork until crumbly. Sprinkle the streusel on top of the uncooked cake.
2. Bake the cake in the oven for about 25 minutes. When the streusel topping is nice and golden, your cake is ready. We know it's hard, but make sure to let it cool off before serving.

SALTED PEANUT BUTTER BROWNIES

Makes: *8 servings* | Time: *40 min*

This recipe is versatile. You can use the base brownie to add almond instead of peanut butter. You can leave out the salt and add raspberries or chopped nuts. However, we highly recommend trying our recommended combination at least once. Peanut butter, chocolate, and salt? Come on. Jackpot!

INGREDIENTS FOR BROWNIES

1 cup (125 g) all-purpose flour

½ cup (55 g) cocoa powder

¾ cup (120 g) brown sugar

¼ teaspoon baking powder

½ cup (120 g) sweetened vegan yogurt

½ cup (125 ml) rice milk

1 tablespoon canola oil

ADDITIONAL INGREDIENTS

¼ cup (70 g) peanut butter

1 sprinkle salt

INSTRUCTIONS

1. Preheat the oven to 400°F/200°C.
2. Mix the all-purpose flour, cocoa powder, brown sugar, and baking powder in a large mixing bowl. Add in the yogurt, rice milk, and canola oil and whisk until combined.
3. Transfer the brownie batter into a loaf pan lined with parchment paper.
4. Heat the peanut butter in a small pot over low heat until melted. Pour the peanut butter over the brownie batter and make swirls with a knife.
5. Bake the brownies in the oven for 20 to 25 minutes until the top is crackly.
6. Let them cool off, then cut them into 8 brownies. Sprinkle with salt and enjoy them all.

APPLE FRITTER RINGS WITH ALMOND MAPLE DIPPING SAUCE

Makes: *10–12 fritters* | Time: *35 min*

We're not sure if the old "An apple a day keeps the doctor away" saying also counts if those apples come in the form of fritters, but that won't stop us from trying! Our vegan apple fritter rings are easy to make and such sweet comfort treats! Don't forget to dip your fritters in our finger-licking good almond maple sauce (otherwise known as liquid gold). Yeah, it's that good.

INGREDIENTS

1 apple (e.g., a slightly sweet apple like Pink Lady)

1 cup (125 g) all-purpose flour

1 teaspoon baking powder

1 teaspoon white sugar

⅓ cup (160 ml) plant-based milk (e.g., rice coconut milk)

⅓ cup (160 ml) sparkling water

oil for frying

1 tablespoon white almond butter

1 teaspoon maple syrup

3 teaspoons water

powdered sugar to sprinkle on top

INSTRUCTIONS

1. Peel the apple and remove the core with an apple corer or knife and cut the apple into 10 to 12 rings.
2. Combine the flour, baking powder, and sugar in a bowl. Add in the plant-based milk and sparkling water and whisk together. Dip each apple ring into the batter. The batter should stick to the apple, but it shouldn't be too thick. Add more water if the batter is too thick or more flour if it's too runny.
3. Heat the frying oil in a pot (just enough so that the apple rings can swim in the oil) to 350°F/175°C. Fry each battered apple ring for 3 to 4 minutes until golden and crispy. If they brown too quickly, your oil is too hot. In that case, reduce the heat a bit.
4. Transfer the fried apple rings to a paper towel to remove excess oil.
5. Whisk together the white almond butter, maple syrup, and water to make the dipping sauce.
6. Sprinkle powdered sugar over the fried apple fritter rings and serve the almond maple dipping sauce on the side. Yum!

CHURROS WITH CHOCOLATE DIPPING SAUCE

Makes: *15 churros* | Time: *55 min*

Everybody loves churros. We've modeled our churro recipe after the original Spanish churro, which is made with simple ingredients and served with an utterly glorious chocolate sauce.

INGREDIENTS

½ cup water

1 tablespoon + 3 tablespoons white sugar (make sure it's vegan!), divided

1 pinch of salt

1 tablespoon coconut oil

1 cup (125 g) all-purpose flour

oil for frying

3 tablespoons white sugar

½ teaspoon cinnamon powder

¼ cup chocolate chips (or baking chocolate)

1 teaspoon coconut oil

INSTRUCTIONS

1. In a pot, heat the water, 1 tablespoon sugar, salt, and coconut oil until the sugar has dissolved. Take the pot off the heat and add in the flour. Stir to combine. Let mixture cool down until cold enough to touch.
2. Fill the churro dough into a piping bag with a star tip. Pipe 5-inch ropes of dough onto parchment paper.
3. Heat the frying oil in a pot (just enough so that the churros can swim; make sure there's enough room in the pot to prevent it from spilling over) to 350°F/175°C, and carefully add the churros (work in batches). Let them fry for 3 to 4 minutes until golden and crisp, then transfer the churros onto a paper towel to remove excess oil.
4. Combine the remaining sugar and cinnamon powder in a deep plate. Coat the churros with the sugar.
5. Heat the chocolate chips and coconut oil in a double boiler until melted to make the chocolate dipping sauce. Serve a side of chocolate dipping sauce with the churros!

COCONUT PANNA COTTA

Makes: *4 servings* | Time: *30 min + 4 hours chilling time*

Rejoice, pudding lovers! This coconut panna cotta is the perfect alternative to an otherwise dairy-loaded dessert. With agar powder being the perfect substitute for gelatin you have all the possibilities in the world. We topped our coconut panna cotta with a ridiculously good almond butter sauce and fresh berries—a perfect treat for hot summer days.

INGREDIENTS

12 oz. (400 ml) full-fat coconut milk

¾ teaspoon agar powder

¼ cup (60 g) white sugar (make sure it's vegan!)

2 tablespoons white almond butter

1 tablespoon maple syrup

1 tablespoon water

fresh blueberries or raspberries

INSTRUCTIONS

1. In a pot, heat the coconut milk, agar powder, and white sugar.
2. Bring it a boil, then reduce the heat and let it simmer for 2 to 3 minutes.
3. Pour it into your dishes and let it cool off before placing it in the fridge for at least 4 hours. (You could also make this the day before and leave it in the refrigerator overnight. This is what I did.)
4. Whisk the white almond butter, maple syrup, and water until smooth to make the almond butter sauce.
5. Top the coconut panna cotta with the almond butter sauce and fresh berries.

THANKS

First and foremost, we want to thank the blog readers of ElephantasticVegan.com. A cookbook (and a second one!) would never have been possible without you.

Thank you, Nicole, and the whole Skyhorse publishing team for believing in us even though we are on the other side of the world.

A big thanks to all of our friends and family, who bravely tasted what we came up in the kitchen.

We also want to thank all vegans, future vegans, and vegan hopefuls who are trying to eat more plant-based meals. The vegan movement wouldn't exist without you.

Thank you, dear reader, for buying this book—or maybe somebody gifted it to you, then thanks to them for buying. We really hope you enjoy reading and cooking from *Cravings Made Vegan* as much as we enjoyed writing it!

NOTES

NOTES

NOTES

NOTES

NOTES

NOTES

NOTES

NOTES

CONVERSION CHARTS

METRIC AND IMPERIAL CONVERSIONS

(These conversions are rounded for convenience)

Ingredient	Cups/Tablespoons/ Teaspoons	Ounces	Grams/Milliliters
Butter	1 cup/ 16 tablespoons/ 2 sticks	8 ounces	230 grams
Cheese, shredded	1 cup	4 ounces	110 grams
Cornstarch	1 tablespoon	0.3 ounce	8 grams
Cream cheese	1 tablespoon	0.5 ounce	14.5 grams
Flour, all-purpose	1 cup/1 tablespoon	4.5 ounces/0.3 ounce	125 grams/8 grams
Flour, whole wheat	1 cup	4 ounces	120 grams
Fruit, dried	1 cup	4 ounces	120 grams
Fruits or veggies, chopped	1 cup	5 to 7 ounces	145 to 200 grams
Fruits or veggies, puréed	1 cup	8.5 ounces	245 grams
Honey, maple syrup, or corn syrup	1 tablespoon	0.75 ounce	20 grams
Liquids: cream, milk, water, or juice	1 cup	8 fluid ounces	240 milliliters
Oats	1 cup	5.5 ounces	150 grams
Salt	1 teaspoon	0.2 ounces	6 grams
Spices: cinnamon, cloves, ginger, or nutmeg (ground)	1 teaspoon	0.2 ounce	5 milliliters
Sugar, brown, firmly packed	1 cup	7 ounces	200 grams
Sugar, white	1 cup/1 tablespoon	7 ounces/0.5 ounce	200 grams/12.5 grams
Vanilla extract	1 teaspoon	0.2 ounce	4 grams

OVEN TEMPERATURES

Fahrenheit	Celsius	Gas Mark
225°	110°	¼
250°	120°	½
275°	140°	1
300°	150°	2
325°	160°	3
350°	180°	4
375°	190°	5
400°	200°	6
425°	220°	7
450°	230°	8

INDEX

N

O

P